CONSPIRACY OF KINDNESS

Conspiracy of Kindness

A Refreshing New Approach to Sharing the Love of Jesus With Others

10th Anniversary Edition

STEVE SJOGREN

Servant Publications
Ann Arbor, Michigan

Vine Books is an imprint of Servant Publications
especially designed to serve evangelical Christians.

Servant Publications Mission Statement

We are dedicated to publishing books that spread the gospel of Jesus Christ,
help Christians to live in accordance with that gospel, promote renewal in the
church, and bear witness to Christian unity.

Scripture passages used in this work are taken from *The New King James
Version,* copyright 1979, 1982, Thomas Nelson, Inc. Publishers.

Published by Servant Publications
P.O. Box 8617
Ann Arbor, Michigan 48107

www.servantpub.com

Cover design by Multnomah Graphics/Printing

03 04 05 06   10 9 8 7 6 5 4 3 2 1

Printed in the United States of America
ISBN 1-56955-334-3

Library of Congress Cataloging-in-Publication Data

Sjogren, Steve, 1955-
    Conspiracy of kindness : a refreshing new approach to sharing the love of
Jesus with others / Steve Sjogren.
       p. cm.
    Includes bibliographical references.
    ISBN 1-56955-334-3 (pbk. : alk. paper)
    1. Evangelistic work. 2. Kindness—Religious aspects–Christianity. I. Title.
    BV3793 .S486 2003
    269'.2—dc21
                                                                2002191046

DEDICATION

To my wife, Janie—you are lovely and talented. Thanks for showing me the patience and grace of God along the way.

To my mom, Glenna—thanks for having and sharing one of the largest hearts on the planet.

To the people of Vineyard of Cincinnati—thanks for embodying God's love, acceptance, and forgiveness. Your hearts have shaped my life.

ACKNOWLEDGMENTS

The concepts presented in this book come from the combined influences of many friends. Their lives have rubbed off on me. Brent Rue had the idea of the first free car wash and embodied the values of servant evangelism. John Wimber mentored me, and he expressed better than anyone what I believe about practical Christianity. Though both are now gone, I continue to be challenged by their wonderful lives. Thank you Kenn Gulliksen for giving me a chance in the ministry and for living in the power of the conspiracy of kindness. I'm grateful for the motivational and editorial help I received from Teresa Cleary, Lynda Sims, Chris Barker, Dave Workman, and Ken Wilson. Thanks, guys, for keeping me on track! Tom Philippi (Mr. Graphics-o-rama), you were always ready in season and out of season with your ideas.

CONTENTS

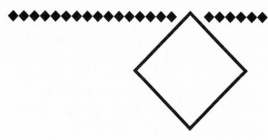

AN INTRODUCTION TO KINDNESS

"Kindness is a language which the dumb can speak, the deaf can understand."
—C.N. Bovee

CHRISTIANS IN AMERICA HAVE LONG been preoccupied with possible conspiracies against the church. Since coming to Christ in 1974, I have heard of at least ten such plots, theories which reflect various levels of creativity and credibility. One widespread rumor was started by an evangelist who claimed to be a former member of the Illuminati, a satanic cult bent on infiltrating the church. This man became discredited overnight when his story was proved to be influenced by LSD.

Another Christian conspiracy revolved around Madalyn Murray O'Hair, a vocal proponent of atheism. O'Hair supposedly had launched a secret campaign with the Federal Communications

Commission to get Christian broadcasting off the air. A couple of times a year someone approached me for permission to circulate a petition to stop this action. When I called the FCC to investigate, I discovered something interesting. To their knowledge no such campaign has *ever* existed, yet they have been receiving petitions from zealous Christians for the past thirty-some years!

The conspiracy theory I've heard about most often concerns the logo of Procter and Gamble, Cincinnati's largest and oldest company. The image depicts a crescent moon and several stars. Coined in the 1800s, it represents the thirteen original colonies, yet many Christians over the years have claimed that this company logo stands for the occult. No matter how often Procter and Gamble expresses its true intention, the rumors continue. Some fear-mongers claim that any naive persons who would dare use Crest toothpaste are thereby supporting the New Age movement and exposing themselves to possible demon possession! The truth is, the only thing anyone will get from using Crest is clean teeth.

I believe there have been few authentic conspiracies against the church, yet we can all bet the family farm that such stories will continue to thrive. But my point in this book isn't to stand atop a soapbox. In fact, one conspiracy really *is* going on today, but not one most of us can readily see. It has gone on quietly, almost unnoticed, at work in the hearts of millions of people without their knowledge. This movement dates back almost two thousand years, drawing unwitting outsiders toward a faith which they haven't consciously embraced. Furthermore, agents of this conspiracy can be found just about everywhere. They are among us, possibly sitting right beside us in church pews. Even some pastors are involved in this secret movement.

Before you type up a petition, I should tell you that this conspiracy is a godly one. Paul spoke of it in his letter to the Romans: "God's kindness is meant to lead you to repentance" (Rom 2:4, RSV). This book is all about that conspiracy—a *conspiracy of kindness.*

God is seeking to enter the heart of every person on this planet, but he faces a significant obstacle to his conspiracy. The problem has never been the message; we have that straight, for the most part. Neither is God's problem the lack of an audience; plenty of people need to hear good news. His problem is the reluctant army he calls the Church. God is looking for people who are willing to participate in acts of love and kindness to those outside of their present circle. He is looking for people who believe that a humble demonstration of love plants a seed of eternity in the hearts of others that will blossom into faith in Christ.

The strategy of this conspiracy operates on the premise that God is passionately in love with unbelievers. As dynamic seeds of kindness are planted in their hearts, the Holy Spirit will pursue them. We are the sowers of those seeds of love. God is the farmer who oversees the entire process.

I certainly do not intend to criticize anyone who is sharing the gospel in other ways. I believe that all honest approaches to evangelism work if we just keep at them. I encourage you to share the gospel *more* with your world, using whatever approach works for you. Clearly the state of evangelism today doesn't demand a *few* good ideas but a *hundred*.

This book compiles the observations and lessons that I and my congregation have learned over the past several years as we have sought to share the good news throughout the city of Cincinnati. I believe that you will be encouraged by the story of what has happened here. Many of these ideas will be new to you. I hope that you can see past the newness and resist the temptation to reject whatever may differ from your established ways of viewing evangelism.

What approach will capture the attention of the non-Christian society around us? I believe that the message of the gospel must be *spoken* and *shown* to the watching world. Surveys and studies indicate that approximately 10 percent of Christians are naturally gifted in the ministry of evangelism. In this book I hope to present a way of reaching the unchurched that can be done easily by the other 90 percent.

In our search for greater effectiveness, we cannot retreat from sharing the message of the gospel. The only negotiable point is

what *approach* we should take. Lowering the entrance requirements to faith in Jesus in order to make the gospel message more
palatable will ultimately backfire on the church and rob the
gospel of its power. We don't want to tamper with the *what* of
the gospel message, but we do need to examine the *how*.

A great message doesn't count for much unless we have an
audience that is listening. Christian researcher George Barna
wrote a powerful booklet entitled "We Have Seen the Future:
The Demise of Christianity in Los Angeles County."[1] In spite of
the appearance of large and very visible churches, he states that
the local church has gradually ceased to influence the secular
community around them. Barna warns that if change doesn't
occur soon, the church in Los Angeles will emit zero influence
on the surrounding world—a pattern which could be repeated
across the nation.

My goal is to present a new vision and a simple strategy for
sharing the message of Jesus' love in a way that will change
people's lives forever. My aim is to stir up in you a heart to obey
God by sharing the good news with those around you. I pray that
these ideas will fuel your courage to step out of your safety zone
and begin to meet the needs of a desperate and hurting world.

Several years ago I began to explore evangelism in a way that
was new to me. After helping to start churches in two previous
cities, my wife Janie and I thought we had a handle on how to do
it. I spent my first two years in Cincinnati driving a school bus
and sharing my desire to launch a new church. After telling over
one thousand people about the kind of church we envisioned, we
held our first Sunday celebration. A grand total of thirty-seven
attended—a rejection rate of about 97 percent!

We recently celebrated our seventeenth anniversary as a
Sunday morning church with over six thousand people attending
five weekend celebrations. We have launched fifteen other
churches in the Cincinnati-Dayton area, with plans for an eventual thirty. Last year these area churches touched well over five
hundred thousand people with the love of God in a tangible way.

As you begin to reach out to your city with deeds of kindness, I would be particularly interested in hearing about new projects which have worked well for you. I regularly include motivational stories in a quarterly evangelism newsletter directed to leaders of kindness outreaches. The best way to reach me is via e-mail at sjogren@cincyvineyard.com. I would love to hear from you!

WHO ANSWERS GOD'S MAIL?

*"Kind words can be short and easy to speak
but their echoes are truly endless."*
—Mother Teresa

*"Keep on sowing your seed, for you never know
which will grow—perhaps it all will."*
—Ecclesiastes 11:6

O N A TYPICAL HOT, HUMID, summer day in Cincinnati, Joe Delaney and his eight-year-old son were in the backyard playing catch. As the two lobbed the ball back and forth, Joe could tell something was on Jared's mind. At first they talked about Reds baseball, friends, and summer vacation. Then the conversation took a more serious turn, and Joe felt like a backyard ballplayer who suddenly found himself in the major leagues.

"Dad, is there a God?"

Joe had the same helpless feeling he experienced on the high school baseball team when he lost sight of a fly ball in the blazing sun. He didn't know whether to move forward, backward, or just stay put. A string of trite answers raced through his mind. In the end Joe opted for honesty. "I don't know, Jared," he replied as the ball landed solidly in his glove.

Joe's agnosticism failed to stifle his son's curiosity. Jared dug a little deeper. "If there is a God, how would you know him?"

"I really have no idea, Jared. I only went to church a couple of times when I was a kid, so I don't know a lot about these kinds of things."

Jared seemed deep in thought for a few minutes as the game of catch continued. Suddenly, he headed for the house. "I'll be right back," he yelled over his shoulder. "I have to get something." Jared soon returned with a mylar helium balloon fresh from the circus along with a pen and an index card.

"Jared, what in the world are you doing?" Joe asked.

"I'm going to send a message to God—airmail," the boy earnestly replied.

Before Joe could protest, his son had started writing. "Dear God," Jared wrote on the index card, "if you are real and if you are there, send people who know you to Dad and me."

Joe kept his mouth shut, not wanting to dampen his son's enthusiasm. *This is silly,* he thought as he helped Jared fasten the card to the balloon's string. *But God, I hope you're watching,* he added to his silent petition. After Jared let go of the balloon, father and son stood with their faces to the sky and watched it sail away.

Two days later I became part of the answer to this unusual inquiry. Joe and Jared pulled into the free car wash that our church was holding as part of our outreach into the community on this particular Saturday morning. "How much?" Joe asked as he neared the line of buckets, sponges, and hoses.

"It's free," I told him. "No strings attached."

"Really!" Joe exclaimed. He seemed intrigued with the idea of getting something for nothing. "But why are you doing this?"

"We just want to show you God's love in a practical way."

It was as if that simple statement opened a hidden door to Joe's heart. The look on his face was incredible. "Wait a minute!" he practically shouted. "Are you guys Christians?"

"Yeah, we're Christians," I replied.

"Are you the kind of Christians who believe in God?"

I couldn't help but smile. "Yes, we're *that* kind of Christians."

After directing a big grin at Jared, Joe proceeded to tell me the story of releasing the helium balloon with its message only days earlier. "I guess you're the answer to one of the strangest prayers God's ever received," Joe said.

"Dear God, if you are real and if you are there,
send people who know you to Dad and me."

THE POWER OF KINDNESS

Joe and Jared's story is one of the thousands of examples of how servant evangelism works as a conspiracy of kindness. After eight years of demonstrating these practical expressions of God's love to total strangers, it's still a thrill to see their eyes light up when they realize that our deeds of kindness are actually free, with no strings attached. As we serve people in practical ways, their attitudes toward God are affected before they even realize it. During this time I've seen hundreds of individuals like Joe open their hearts to God.

People often ask me to explain servant evangelism in a nutshell. I'm not very good at putting anything in a nutshell, but this is the definition we use in our church: *demonstrating the kindness of God by offering to do some act of humble service with no strings attached.* Let's tear that definition apart, one piece at a time.

Demonstrating the kindness of God. Whenever people see the love of God in action, a hot button is touched deep inside them. I'm convinced they *feel* God's presence and *see* that he's real even though they usually don't know how to respond. Some people seem to even hear something audible from the Lord when we serve them.

Jesus said, "By this all will know that you are my disciples, if you have love for one another" (Jn 13:35). This verse is often interpreted as a call to unity in the Body of Christ. God certainly wants us to love other believers, but Jesus' call goes far beyond those narrow boundaries. He called the disciples to love one another because the world instinctively recognizes us as followers of Jesus when we demonstrate that love for all to see.

By offering to do. The mere offer to serve others holds great power. For example, one of our teams was going from store to store in a large mall in Cincinnati offering to clean their restrooms. When we explain what we are doing the atmosphere around us gets quiet, like the commercial some years ago, "When E.F. Hutton speaks, everybody listens." I admit, it does look rather odd to see a couple of people come up with bucket in hand and make this offer.

One particular Saturday morning, a female shopper couldn't help but eavesdrop when our team asked permission to clean a store's toilet. She later discovered that one of the engineers at her company attends our fellowship and asked him, "What kind of Christians are you who clean toilets to show God's love? This sort of Christianity sparks my interest!"

Often the results of our projects will extend far beyond those we directly touch. When we give away soft drinks, not everyone wants a can. Sometimes just one person in a group of four at a football game would receive a drink, but as they walk away the entire group would read the card and retell the story with an inquisitive look on their faces. This past week we touched about one thousand people in a variety of outreach projects, but the actual number who heard about what we did was much larger, possibly by a factor of two or three. Because the offer of service is so intriguing to people, they tend to tell their friends.

Some act of humble service. Jesus came as the suffering, humble servant. The goal in servant evangelism is to shine the spotlight on God's kingdom by coming in the spirit of Jesus. God understood that humility is one of the traits that gets the attention of the human race. As we give away deeds of humility we bring a similar influence into the world. In recent years we have been operating under a new assumption: *It is normal for Christians to serve those outside the church.* As we allow Jesus to love others through us, we will find great joy in serving.

Humility seems to make sense to everyone except veteran churchgoers. Jesus' lowly estate threw a curve ball to the religious leaders of his day. They expected him to appear as victorious Lord of Lords and King of Kings. Of course, Jesus is coming the second time in manifest power and authority, but he came the first time in humility. Today, it seems little has changed. While we look high and low for effective approaches that will touch the world around us with God's love, the most obvious one is often overlooked. Doing humble acts of service causes the world to notice our lives and to listen to our message.

With no strings attached. Our service to the community is always free. Many people offer to donate to our "cause," but we always refuse any repayment. To receive money for what we do would lessen the impact of our services. Free service offers a picture of the grace of God, a priceless gift which can never be repaid.

Last fall one small group went out on several Saturday mornings raking leaves. One lady was overjoyed at our offer and said, "You've just saved me a *big* job." With six to eight people it doesn't take long to knock off a small yard, but that same job would have taken her hours to do alone.

When we began to leave, she wrote out a check for our services. We had said earlier we were doing this for free, but our words hadn't registered with her. We continued to load our rakes and bags into the back of a pickup truck and she was still trying to stick her check in our pockets. It was quite a sight—right out of a Laurel and Hardy episode! Even as we were driving away, this woman was still waving her arms with her check in hand.

Free service offers a picture of the grace of God, a priceless gift which can never be repaid.

♦♦♦

About a week later she got the better of us by sending a check in the mail with a short note, "I told you I wanted to pay for your raking my lawn! Please use this for whatever." We kept the letter and gave the money to our ministry to the needy.

How Does Servant Evangelism Work?

I witnessed the effectiveness of servant evangelism at a recent evangelism conference held in Houston. I was one of several speakers offering different ideas for spreading the good news. My part was to teach on how to step out in simple expressions of God's love to outsiders. A friend of mine, a pastor who is gifted in speaking to strangers about Christ, spoke about sharing the gospel through friendship, prayer for the sick, and open air preaching—whatever seemed to fit each person. After talking about evangelism for a couple of days, we spent the last day actually going out to do it.

For the faint of heart, we did a free car wash, free windshield washing, and a food-giveaway to single mothers. For the more courageous, we offered more traditional approaches: going door to door, taking surveys, and preaching at a local park frequented by joggers. Unfortunately, the joggers paid no attention to what was being said. Not long after the preaching team began, the Houston police showed up to make sure this group had a permit to hold a meeting. Since they didn't, the police asked them to disperse. The group was disappointed, though some later admitted they were a little relieved. "At least now I don't have to talk to strangers," they reasoned.

As they started to leave, one lady announced that she had an idea, hopped into her car, and drove off. Ten minutes later she pulled up with twenty dozen Popsicles! She explained, "I just thought that there was probably no law against giving out Popsicles without a permit." The group discovered that joggers who aren't necessarily interested in listening to a stranger preaching at them are completely open to talking to a stranger offering them free refreshments.

Within twenty minutes all of the Popsicles were gone. Some joggers took the Popsicles and went their way without much conversation. Others were curious: "Why are you being so nice to me? I don't even know you." "What kind of Christians are you guys anyway?"

These were not difficult questions to answer. In fact, the former preachers were thrilled to have people asking any questions at all. One man took a Popsicle and asked the "why" question with a stunned look on his face. When he was told this was to show God's love in a practical way, he began to tell his life's story to the Christian he had just met.

The case of the preachers turned Popsicle-distributors illustrates something I've seen time and again: servant evangelism works. People on the receiving end of these simple acts of kindness come away with a more positive impression of Christianity than they previously had. With regular frequency, these deeds also open a door to deeper communication about the gospel. And those who engage in this approach to sharing God's love with strangers don't come away feeling like they've been put through a meat grinder.

Servant evangelism is one method—not the only method, nor

necessarily the best one for every situation. And like any other approach, it simply doesn't work apart from the agency of the Holy Spirit who is the only true evangelist. Its effectiveness may vary from one cultural setting to another and there may well come a time when it has outlived its usefulness.

Nevertheless, in a society where other forms of sharing the gospel often meet a great deal of resistance—one which feels it's heard too much "God-talk" and not seen enough "God-activity" —servant evangelism seems to be a fruitful way for Christians to share God's love with their community. Our experience in Cincinnati has shown us that evangelism must contain the right words, but that those words must *follow* the demonstration of the love of God. The following equation states how this approach works:

◆◆◆

Servant evangelism =
deeds of love + words of love + adequate time

◆◆◆

Following this sequence of *deeds* of love before *words* of love practically communicates that the experience of God's love precedes the understanding of that love. The scriptural record of his activity among the human race reflects this pattern. God does something wonderful with people, and only later—sometimes years later—do they understand or make sense of what he did. The apostles experienced the works of Jesus for three years and then spent decades making sense out of those works. As recorded in Acts 2, the early church experienced the coming of the Holy Spirit in power, but these same men wrote and applied this event for decades.

Deeds of love. God's love must be communicated from person to person, not just from page to person. If his love could be sent through printed information alone, we could simply flood our cities with gospel tracts and then rest assured that we have done our part. Deeds of love allow us to sneak into the hearts of those we serve. Even though people aren't conscious of what's happening, they are welcoming us and the God we represent into the fortress of their hearts. Deeds of love aren't enough on their own to bring someone to Christ, but they do create "phone wires" for transmitting the spoken message.

Words of love. Deeds of kindness get people's attention and often cause them to ask us questions. Instead of having a forced presentation of the gospel to people who really aren't interested in what we have to say, we find people are curious and ask us to explain what we're about after we've served them. Then we can present the message which is vital in bringing someone to Christ without taking a sales approach.

When we do speak we must be sensitive to the level of receptivity of each person and explain the words of God's love in whatever way the hearer can understand. These words are the cognitive or conscious element of our evangelism. If we don't follow our actions with words, they will only know that we are nice people, not that God loves them.

Adequate time. We need to allow time for deeds and words of love to have their effect on the hearts of people. If we are allowing the Holy Spirit to do his work in his way and in his timing, we must not demand instantaneous results. We can be assured that God will not allow any seed he has sown to come back without bearing fruit (Is 55:11), but he typically works over a prolonged period of time to bring sinners to himself. As we allow adequate time for seeds of love to take root, we put the expectation for results on the right spot: the Holy Spirit.

We might ask, "How long does it take for someone to come to Christ?" The only right answer to that question is, "It takes a unique amount of time for each person." One day while attending Bible school in Los Angeles, I was walking by a city park and saw a young Chicano wearing the attire of a gang member. The

Holy Spirit spoke to me and said, "If you ask that guy to accept Christ, he will say yes." After arguing with myself—*That can't be the Lord's will ... this guy is a gang member!*—I decided to obey anyway and struck up a conversation. I happened to have a Spanish edition of the Four Spiritual Laws in my New Testament. After talking with him for fifteen minutes, to my utter surprise, this tough-looking teen prayed with me to accept Christ!

That young man's immediate response represents the exception rather than the rule. In my early Christian life, if people didn't respond to the gospel I would apply my standard motto: "Increase the pressure!" Frankly, that approach to evangelism resembles a practice used by many cults called "love bombing." Great attention is given to prospective converts for four to six weeks—supposedly as a means for showing love. It often turns out to be a fake love, just a sales tactic to convince newcomers to join. If someone refuses, he or she is dropped like a hot potato.

God relates to each person we contact as individuals. Our call to share the good news means loving people until they come around to relationship with Jesus Christ—regardless of how much time it takes. Those who don't give the Holy Spirit adequate time to do heart surgery will hinder his role of ripening the seeds we may have helped to plant. Our job is to bring them the love of Jesus with all the grace he provides.

WHY DOES SERVANT EVANGELISM WORK?

I believe servant evangelism works because it respects certain important factors that influence the effectiveness of evangelism in our society. Let's consider these key factors one by one.

Sharing the good news is not a one-shot deal. American Christians tend to view evangelism as a one-shot deal—a "let 'em have it while we've got their attention" blast from both barrels of a shotgun loaded with Scripture. Sharing the good news of Jesus Christ with our neighbors is a *process* rather than a *project*. Like people everywhere, those joggers in Houston were on their own journey toward or away from God. Some were already friends with God, some were alienated children, and others were already well on their way to discovering God.

American Christians tend to view evangelism as a one-shot deal—a "let 'em have it while we've got their attention" blast from both barrels of a shotgun loaded with Scripture.

Paul states: "I have planted, Apollos watered, but God gave the increase" (1 Cor 3:6). Implied in his words is the notion of evangelism as a process, a sort of spiritual continuum that includes every human being. Paul's view of evangelism is quite unlike our American mindset which tends to focus on the "harvesting" aspect of soul-winning rather than the planting part.

Opening hearts which have long been closed to God's love isn't something that normally happens quickly. Dr. Paul Benjamin discovered a common pattern after interviewing hundreds of people who had come to Christ in the early 1970s. In his book, *The Equipping Ministry,* he states that the average person requires five significant encounters with the gospel before accepting Jesus Christ as Savior.[1] Dr. Benjamin defines a "significant encounter" as one in which a person actually *hears* the message of God's love in such a way that it registers in his or her heart. We see in this conversion pattern that it is one thing to *send* a message and quite another to see that message make a lasting impact on someone's life.

I can remember at least five significant encounters that led to my own decision to receive Jesus as Lord and Savior. First, after attending a Doobie Brothers rock concert, someone handed me a tract about God's love. Even though it was poorly written, the Lord used that brief message to get my attention. Not long afterward, a second touch occurred when I noticed that a barber had put a before and after photo of himself in his storefront window, along with a sign claiming that Jesus had made a difference in his life. Third, I picked up an issue of *Time* magazine which covered the story of the Jesus People movement in Southern California.

A fourth experience came in high school when I nearly drowned at a lake in Northern Arizona. I had heard that drowning victims see their life pass before them. Mine did. That experience scared me enough to focus my attention on questions of life, death, eternity, and God. Not long after I began to ask these questions I met a couple of Christians who told me their story of coming to Christ. And not long after that fifth touch I asked Jesus to enter my heart.

My own experience underscores my belief that the lion's share of bringing the good news involves the planting and watering of seeds of love through simple acts of kindness. We must be willing to plant and water before we will begin to see the harvest.

The first 90 percent of bearing witness to God's love is "precognitive." The Holy Spirit is doing a deep work in the *heart* of the person being drawn to the Lord. It is not so much a matter of sharing *information* as sharing *love*. We often plant these seeds of love long before people have consciously considered the claims of Christ. The Holy Spirit—the "Hound of Heaven"—is always busy doing a deep work in the human heart long before a person can give language to God's action.

Anyone can do simple acts of kindness. For most Christians doing evangelism is a lot like going to the dentist: no one really enjoys doing it, but it has to be done every once in a while. They often equate "being obedient to God" with doing something that is distasteful, unnatural, and even contrary to their nature. In other words, if preaching at the park scares me to death, then it must be God's perfect will!

Some of those who went to the park in Houston admitted later on that they went along just because they wanted to "obey the Lord." When they switched from preaching to simply offering relief from the elements to those who jogged by, every person on the team felt encouraged. They realized this was something they could do easily. Failing at an assignment like this is almost impossible. Worst case scenario: the Popsicles melt because people aren't hot and thirsty enough.

I've found that people are often more comfortable *doing* for others than they are simply *talking* to them. The reported number-one fear of Americans is talking to strangers! When they assume they're being asked to do the very thing they most fear in life, it's no wonder so many Christians cringe at the prospect of evangelism.

On the other hand, serving is a reasonable task to ask of the average "coward" in the Body of Christ. I believe that most of us are cowards when it comes to sharing the gospel with strangers. When using these simple approaches to touching others, timid Christians come to realize they have nothing to lose. That's a good feeling.

For most Christians doing evangelism is a lot like going to the dentist: no one really enjoys doing it, but it has to be done every once in a while.

Servant evangelism is a low-risk venture. It doesn't take a great deal of gifting, money, or even boldness to influence large numbers of people. For several years we have been looking for simple ways to influence shoppers at local grocery stores, a natural gathering place for many Americans on Saturday mornings. During the winter we regularly give away fresh brewed coffee. It's easy to attract people from our church to participate in this kind of project. After all, who *can't* pour a cup of coffee!

Doing acts of kindness is "high grace." When we step out to do simple deeds of love, God usually shows up to bless our efforts. His presence is often tangible. Time and again we have seen him convert our simple acts of service into powerful and unforgettable seeds planted in people's hearts.

During the Christmas season we provide free gift wrapping at several area malls as a part of our outreach efforts. Our refusal to accept money shocks many of our customers who are used to paying for everything. One afternoon, a couple of volunteers were manning our wrapping booth when a woman brought in a couple of presents. As they wrapped her gifts, they explained to her that they were doing this to show her God's love in a practical way. This woman asked if we were the kind of Christians that believed in "healing prayer." When they answered yes, she asked if they would pray for her back. She explained that she was an airline stewardess and had been off work for some weeks due to a lower back problem. With a mall full of people walking by, they prayed a simple healing prayer. After a few moments, she noted with an amazed look that her lower back was completely numb. The pain had completely gone away.

Sometimes God's grace appears in a powerful sort of way, as with the stewardess. At other times he is present in more subtle ways, as with the joggers. Whenever we serve, each person is influenced in some unique way by the personalized touch of the Holy Spirit. Instead of telling the gospel in a forced way, we simply answer the questions others initiate.

Evangelism hits home when it begins with acceptance. Houston, Texas, is sometimes called the "Buckle of the Bible Belt." The prolific number of churches in that city prompts people to think of it as a bastion of conservative Christianity. To those outside the scope of the church, however, conservative Christianity is not always seen in a positive light. In fact, they often perceive believers as resembling Dana Carvey's "Church Lady" on *Saturday Night Live.*

One skit centers around a church potluck supper where a single mom apologizes to the pastor for the small dish which she has to offer. He tells her, "Whatever you can bring is good enough for this dinner." Moments later the Church Lady arrives carrying an elaborate casserole that everyone makes a fuss over. She points out to all present that she spent hours preparing this dish. Because it is so enormous, the single mom feels inferior. In her mind the Church Lady had scored because everyone has once again recognized that she is better than most people. The skit ends with the Church Lady doing her "superior dance," strutting about with her head bobbing and her hands on her hips. The American public finds this character funny because she embodies the way many outsiders perceive Christians.

Some of the joggers in the park may have perceived the preaching group as pushy, judgmental, self-righteous, and rejecting of others who didn't think exactly the same way. When we use the phrase "the *Bible* says," we don't necessarily get the immediate attention of the world, and we certainly don't get their immediate respect.

For centuries Christians have been identified through a variety of badges which vary from one culture to another. At times they have been known by the length of their hair (or lack of hair), crosses around their neck, wearing plain clothing or dark garments, getting rid of their TVs, or avoiding certain foods. All of those "signs" are cultural identifiers, statements to their particular generation about their own personal faith.

According to the Bible, only one true and lasting sign identifies us as followers of Jesus through all times and cultures. The world around us recognizes the same sign that Jesus pointed to: our love. "By this all men will know that you are my disciples, if you have love for one another" (Jn 13:35, RSV). This love must spill over from the walls of our churches and out into the community in significant ways if we are going to make any lasting impact. It seems people don't necessarily remember what they are *told* of God's love, but they never forget what they have *experienced* of God's love.

We cannot love people without first accepting them. A group of young people from our church have been reaching out for several years to the patrons of an alternative dance club in the downtown Cincinnati area. Those who regularly attend this club present a scary appearance with their shaved heads, tattoos, and black leather clothes. One young guy named Paul was amazed that Christians would polish his black boots for free just to demonstrate the love of God. He began to spend time with this group of Christians and eventually came to church with them.

It seems people don't necessarily remember what they are told of God's love, but they never forget what they have experienced of God's love.

When these Christians first met Paul they were unaware that he had been convicted of a felonious crime and was weeks away from starting a four-year prison sentence. While serving time Paul began to consider the actions of these Christians. He felt like he had encountered real love because they seemed to love him as much as they loved one another, even though he wasn't a believer. That seed of kindness—which began when his boots were shined for free—sprang up after several months of confinement when Paul asked Jesus Christ to enter his life. Hearing about God's love was important to him, but the power of acceptance proved to him that God's love is real.

Evangelism must overcome a credibility gap. We live in a day when the church's credibility is at an all-time low. When we step up to bat in sharing the good news with the unchurched public, we already have two strikes against us. Billy Graham saw the world's summary of the church during an anti-Vietnam rally some years ago when a student held up a sign which read, "JESUS *YES!* CHURCH *NO!*" Even today, that slogan accurately reflects the feelings and attitudes of many people across our country.

Because of the front-page publicity given to sex and money

scandals involving several visible leaders in the church, many unchurched people feel Christians must earn the right to be heard. Before we share God's *words* of love with a hurting world, we must first be willing to do *deeds* of love with the heart of a servant. We must balance the speaking and the doing of the gospel—the words and the works of God—if we expect to gain an audience with the watching world.

In our attempts to share the gospel, many of us have talked a lot but been weak on demonstration. John Wimber made this important point in his book *Power Evangelism,* when he says, "Jesus both spoke the *words* and did the *works* of the Father."[2] We need to become word-workers, as Wimber encourages.

Mother Teresa brought clarity to the world's viewpoint in this statement: "True acts of love go before God forever as worship to him." Instead of just telling the gospel, we are *bringing* the gospel to people. Our society expects to be preached at by enthusiastic Christians. It is almost shocking to unbelievers when we break that expectation by offering simple, practical demonstrations of God's love.

People often ask us, "Why are you *really* doing this? You want me to join your church, don't you?" Typically we respond with, "You're sure welcome to come to our church, but more than anything we are here because this is the way Jesus walked on the earth. If he were bodily walking the streets of Cincinnati today, Jesus would be showing people the love of God in practical ways. Instead of washing feet he might be washing cars. After all, that's the way people get around these days."

An experience of love opens a person's heart to a message of love. A group of Christians traveled to the summer Olympics in Barcelona hoping to do significant evangelism in the large crowds gathered from around the world. Unfortunately, they received less than an enthusiastic welcome from local officials who informed them that evangelism was specifically not allowed. Instead of reacting negatively to this message, this group of believers went to work meeting whatever practical needs they saw. They began to clean up the streets, empty trash cans, and generally do whatever they could see that needed to be done around the Olympic grounds.

After a few days of watching these Christians, the officials called the Christian leaders in and admitted that they were pretty impressed with the attitude that they had seen displayed. They went on to ask, "What sort of evangelism were you hoping to do, *if* you were allowed?" After the Christian leaders explained themselves, they received the OK to pursue whatever outreach they wanted as long as they kept in touch with the civic officials. What a staggering turnaround, and all because these believers were willing to *be* the good news before they began to *speak* the good news.

Who answers God's mail? Joe and Jared's experience makes it clear that he wants to involve us in the process. God answers his own mail, but he does it through people like you and me, people who are willing to step out and touch others through simple demonstrations of his love. I now see myself as one of the carriers of the Lord's mail. You and I have been called to be a part of God's conspiracy, a conspiracy of kindness aimed at the heart of every person alive today. The easiest entrance point into someone's life is a simple deed done in kindness. In the next chapter, let's look at some of the barriers to getting involved in this conspiracy of kindness.

UNLEARNING THE "E" WORD

*"The heart that breaks open
can contain the whole universe."*
—Joanna Macy

I TAUGHT AT AN ELEMENTARY SCHOOL for two years before I began pastoring full-time. One day while my fourth grade class was playing softball, an enthusiastic boy named Lloyd decided his team would be more likely to win if he were to trip the base runners as they came by. When I caught him sticking out his foot, I benched him for the remainder of the game.

Lloyd was so upset that he called me a few names. "You're nothing but a dirty —," he mumbled under his breath so I couldn't quite catch the word. He wouldn't repeat what he had said to me, so I invited Lloyd to an after-school conference with Mr. Ferguson, the principal—a man who was widely feared among the fourth graders.

Lloyd was still too embarrassed to tell us what he had said. We insisted he come clean and got him to tell us the first letter. Lloyd said it began with an "e." Mr. Ferguson and I looked at each other and silently mouthed, "What terrible curse word begins with an 'e'?" Again we pressed Lloyd to tell us.

"Okay," the boy said, "I called Mr. Sjogren a dirty little *idiot!*" ("ediot," depending on how you spell it). For the rest of that school year, the staff often asked me if I had been called the "e" word lately.

Some words have a tendency to take on an emotional edge after a while. Every so often it's important for us to examine the redefinitions that may have quietly taken place. For example, when many Christians hear the word "prayer," they don't feel encouraged. Rather, they feel like failures. Just about every Christian I know finds it difficult to carry on an effective prayer life. After years of personally struggling with prayer, many of us assume that everyone else who loves Jesus is doing great in that area. Soon the mere mention of the word "prayer" sets off intense feelings of guilt.

"Evangelism" is another one of those emotionally charged words that often sends shivers of guilt running up and down our spines. It registers in us emotionally the way Mr. Ed the talking horse would have said it in the 1960s, with a little vibrato: "Eee-vannnn-gelllll-issssm-uh!" So many of us feel like failures when we try to share our faith—all but the few who can really do it well. That may be the way we feel, but it's not supposed to work that way. Somehow along the way we've become confused about what it means to represent Jesus to the lost world around us.

Everyone agrees that evangelism involves giving away the message of God's love. We agree on the *focus* of our message, but diverge greatly when it comes to deciding *how* that message is to be carried to the world. When I was a new Christian, I was influenced by a confusing hodgepodge of books, tapes, radio Bible teachers, and enthusiastic friends, and blindly adopted others' values as my own. As a result, I had a rocky start in evangelism.

My attempts at sharing the gospel could be divided into three phases: the "shark phase," the "carp phase," and finally the "dolphin phase." (These helpful terms were coined by authors Dudley Lynch and Paul L. Kordis in their book *Strategy of the Dolphin.*[1]) Let's examine the way Christians typically approach evangelism in light of these three possible choices.

*So many of us feel like failures
when we try to share our faith—
all but the few who can really do it well.*

◆◆◆

THE SHARK

Sharks don't just live life, they attack it! They come at life with great aggressiveness, with control as their highest value. Sharks tend to be movers and shakers who love to take over in any project at hand. They're known for getting a lot done but not necessarily without incident. On the downside, sharks tend to traumatize everyone around them with their unfettered aggression. Consequently, they don't always have strong long-term prospects for productivity. Sharks tend to fit the picture of all the worst characteristics of a pushy salesman.

Most of what we think of as "personal evangelism" falls under the shark approach. If we were to conduct a word association test on the average American using the word "evangelist," I believe we would get some telling responses. Many Christians unconsciously take on a certain persona when it comes to doing evangelism. Having become used to an image, we may no longer be sensitive to elements in our behavior that keep unbelievers away from God.

Even though stereotypes of evangelists may be exaggerated, they are often grounded in the truth. Comedians who appear on late-night talk shows often pick up on this caricature. They portray those doing evangelism as angry, pushy, loud (when loud isn't necessary), opinionated, militant, Southern-accented (even if from Des Moines), sweaty (frequently dabbing forehead with monogrammed, white handkerchief), someone who can make a two-syllable word out of a one-syllable word ("Gaaaa-duhhh" for "God"), unreasonable, negative (emphasizing the judgment of God), and simplistic in their thinking (black-and-white terms that are overgeneralized).

This description fit me to a tee at an earlier point in my Christian life. From the first day of my conversion, I wanted *everyone* to meet this Jesus who had transformed my life. I began to do evangelism without the aid of any books or teaching. The only model I had was one provided by the older people who attended local holiness prayer meetings: hold meetings, give testimonies, and call people forward to give their lives to Christ.

After being away at school for a year, I was picked up at the airport by my mom. In the course of the one-hour trip home, I eagerly explained to her everything I knew about the entire message of the Bible from Genesis to Revelation. I was talking so fast I must have sounded like an auctioneer. All Mom could say was, "And it's nice to see you again too, Steve." It must have been difficult hearing a teenager explain the meaning of life.

I spent the first several years of my Christian life seeking to "soul win" everyone in sight. During this time I lived with the view that the world was a very disorderly place. As I saw it, my assignment was to bring it into order by evangelizing. I cornered every relative and friend who would listen for a few minutes and let them have it with both barrels. It wasn't long before I had shell-shocked everyone I knew. After a while when people saw me coming, they would make up excuses like, "I can't talk now, I've got to polish my dog."

Looking back, talking with me must have been as exciting as going to the dentist. What I shared during that time was the truth, but the package in which the message came wrapped was incredibly unloving and insensitive. At that time I was in actuality functioning more as a *soul alienator* than a *soul winner.*

I wouldn't leave home without a handful of tracts. I especially enjoyed putting them in unusual places—like menus in restaurants, magazines in the store racks, even in a roll of toilet paper for the next person in the restroom stall to read! My favorite tracts capitalized on the use of fear to get people's attention. One had a picture of a hearse on the front and read, "You put your own shoes on this morning." Then it read on the inside, "But tonight the undertaker may be taking them off."

After a while when people saw me coming,
they would make up excuses like, "I can't talk now,
I've got to polish my dog."

The goal of the shark's approach to evangelism is confrontation. Once I was out with a group of my friends doing what we called "street witnessing." We would walk up to total strangers and try to share the good news with them. As soon as I had said the words, "Hi, I'm a Christian and I'd like to talk with you for a few minutes," one man turned around and spoke to me while facing in the opposite direction. He said, "I'm going to count to ten. When I finish if you're still standing behind me I'm going to give you a black eye." That was my idea of giving away God's love.

After five years of enthusiastically offending people for the Lord, I could see the fruit of my efforts all around me: I had traumatized most of my friends, relatives, and neighbors. I told myself I was being rejected because I loved God so much, but my victims didn't see any love at all in what I'd done. I had managed to ostracize all of my family and friends in the name of the Lord. Even so, the aggressiveness of the shark model seemed to me to be the only possible gear for bringing Christ to non-Christians. (I think it might be wise to send all new Christians to a remote desert island for the first couple of years of their Christian life to work out their faith and temper their enthusiasm with a measure of wisdom.)

THE CARP

At the opposite extreme of sharks, carp move through life in a lethargic manner. They see themselves as life's victims, too weak to ever function as a change-agent in life. Carp exist on the bottom of the river and live off of food that the other fish have discarded. They have the opposite nature of the aggressive shark. Carp are dropouts from the fight and make it their primary aim in life to seek the safe route and to avoid any sense of responsibility. Carp don't *make* things happen, they *watch* things happen around them and seem to never have any clue as to why life goes as it does.

In terms of evangelism, carp are sometimes former zealots for the Lord, believers who have become discouraged along the way and have given up trying to lead others to Christ because they couldn't take the pressure. These former sharks usually don't consciously decide to take a break from sharing the good news. Many simply don't understand that there is more than one way to bring God's love to the world. Their love for God or people hasn't necessarily grown dim; they've just grown tired of militant evangelism.

I recently spoke with a pastor who had heard about the basic idea of servant evangelism. Wanting to do something unusual for his community in California, he decided to sponsor a free, no-donations-allowed car wash. At that time, a severe drought kept water at a premium, so the pastor had to buy the necessary water. He and a couple of dozen people from the church washed over one hundred cars. In conversation after conversation, the drivers were stunned at this simple act of love.

At the end of the day, the workers gathered to share about various encounters with people from the community. As they did so, this pastor began to weep. He realized that in one three-hour period he had shared the good news of Jesus Christ with more people than in the previous two years combined! I have known this pastor for several years. He is a man with a great love for God and a strong desire to bring people into the kingdom of God. But like many Christians, his life had been carpish for some time. Without a workable model, he was stuck watching the world go by rather than intersecting it with the love of Jesus Christ.

THE DOLPHIN

Dolphins combine the strengths of sharks and carp. These people are enthusiastic and positive about life, yet keep the issue of personal responsibility in proper balance. The dolphin moves through life with a deep sense of purpose, whereas the shark tends to be overly responsible and the carp accomplishes little or nothing. The dolphin has a mission in life, but still has fun on the way to the goal.

In recent years I have sought to live more as a dolphin—proceeding with a clear objective in my evangelism, but also seeking to enjoy life along the way. My new motto is, "Where the Spirit of the Lord is, there is fun!" Deep down I have always been a dolphin. I believe most of us are really dolphins, but when we begin to act like sharks, our message becomes difficult to believe.

We have been trying to teach the youth from our church about approaching evangelism as dolphins. During a weekend conference along with several other churches from the Cincinnati area, the one thousand plus teens and their leaders went out to do personal evangelism. The youth groups showed up unannounced at a large local mall and began to do shark-like evangelism—all of the groups except for the teens from our church. Our youth leaders held back when the other groups dispersed into the mall. They waited to see what needs people might have and then simply tried to meet those needs. The group soon went to work carrying shopping bags, picking up trash on the ground, emptying ashtrays, and cleaning storefront windows for merchants.

When mall personnel asked why they were being so helpful, they responded with our usual reply: "We just want to show you God's love in a practical way." Several lengthy conversations were started with curious bystanders. Before long an irate customer called the police to complain about the more sharkish evangelists. As our youth quietly went about serving in practical ways, the police escorted the other youth groups out to the parking lot.

*I believe most of us are really dolphins,
but when we begin to act like sharks,
our message becomes difficult to believe.*

◆◆◆

As I look at the gospel accounts of the life and ministry of Jesus, I can see that he went from person to person operating as a dolphin. He modeled for us a life that balanced times of intensity with periods of relaxation. Jesus clearly understood who he was and what his call from God entailed. No Scripture better captures his call than the reading from Isaiah 61 which served as the text for Jesus' first sermon, probably spoken at the synagogue where he had grown up.

Those who had watched him grow up were now seated in front of him as Jesus was handed the scroll. "The Spirit of the Lord is upon me, because he has anointed me to preach the gospel to the poor. He has sent me to heal the brokenhearted, to preach deliverance to the captives and recovery of sight to the blind, to set at liberty those who are oppressed, to preach the acceptable year of the Lord" (Lk 4:18-19).

Jesus' audience didn't like what they were hearing. The ministry he described was so different that the synagogue leaders, a predominantly sharkish bunch, became furious. These verses describe evangelism according to Jesus. He *knew* his audience: the broken. They came with different kinds of brokenness, but they all needed God's love in order to be healed. Jesus also knew his approach: simple and direct. In short, *Jesus was a bringer of*

God's love to the broken of the world. That's evangelism, Jesus-style. We are called to bring the good news to the world in just the same way.

THE OLD VERSUS THE NEW

A friend of mine played high school football on one of the most successful teams in Southern California in the 1950s. One of the keys to their success was the way their practice sessions always began on Monday afternoon: with a review of the goals of the game of football. After some warm-up exercises, the coach would call the players to the middle of the field for a basic overview—and I do mean basic. He would start out holding up a football and saying, "This is a football. Notice the shape, feel, size, and color. The object of this game is to carry this ball across the goal line at the opposite end of the field. No points are awarded for running backward or sideways." This award-winning coach would carry on like this for the first few minutes of every Monday's practice. Any player who laughed or didn't pay attention had to run laps as punishment.

Most Christians who set out to do evangelism fail to define their goals beforehand. And not knowing the goal makes it difficult to succeed. For the most part, the contemporary church still uses models of evangelism from a different century. I don't believe it's necessarily true that "old" is bad and "new" is good, but I do think our evangelistic efforts often operate on the premise of "the old is good and the new is suspicious." Many Christians resist new wineskins, including new ways of bringing the gospel to the world. Vance Havner, the often quoted pastoral statesman, maintains that the last seven words of the church will be, "We've never done it that way before."

Traditional models for evangelism typically focus on the special gifting of a few visible evangelists. Anointed communicators such as Jonathan Edwards, Billy Sunday, and R.A. Torrey have played a vital role in bringing the message of Jesus' love into the world. These approaches were very effective at various points in church history, but the society into which the gospel must be spoken has changed tremendously. The outward form of any approach is useful for a season and then eventually wears out. We need to have the insight to retire those methods which have completed their lifespan.

The early days of William Booth's Salvation Army offer a good example of the amazing effectiveness of a type of evangelism that worked at one time but no longer suits modern society. In the latter half of the 1800s, the Salvationists were able to draw in massive crowds from the London streets with marching brass bands. Once the crowd had assembled, open-air preaching would win many to Christ.

Not long ago, I visited Oslo, Norway, where I saw a group of enthusiastic people marching through the streets and calling people to an open-air meeting. What I saw was nearly exactly the same approach that was used some one hundred years ago. What worked as a cutting edge approach to preaching the gospel in 1850 brought little or no response in Oslo that day.

A review of church history reveals predictable patterns in the way groups develop. A particular five-step pattern has been repeated many times. A *man* (or woman) captures something fresh from the heart of the Lord. That person's obedience and application of truth cause *methods* to emerge. As those methods are applied on a broad scale, *momentum* builds. That momentum grows stronger and stronger until a *movement* emerges. After the person who founded the movement dies, the white-hot presence of the Lord eventually cools down. The group continues on, unaware that their methods have lost effectiveness. After all, the movement is still intact and the methods still produce some results.

Typically groups find it difficult to be completely honest about a loss of momentum. They tend to spiritualize what is happening. "The Lord must be teaching us something in this season of unfruitfulness." Of course, the Lord probably is indeed teaching them something, but the group may be operating in a universe of their own making which doesn't require an objective reality to continue. Existing church machinery can become self-perpetuating. The focus shifts from what the Lord *is* doing to reflecting on the glory days—what the Lord *was* doing. Monuments are established, books are written, and the founders become posthumous heroes in the afterglow of what happened "once upon a time."

The focus shifts from what the Lord is doing
to reflecting on the glory days—
what the Lord was doing.

♦♦♦

This five-step cycle suggests that leaders tend to see what they want to see. The church as a whole often loses sight of the modern world. We forget how the people of our generation hear the Christian message. The gospel of Jesus Christ is unchanging, but the trappings of the world around our message is everchanging. In just the same way, the heart of our evangelism remains constant, but the exterior stands in need of continual change in order to communicate effectively to contemporary society.

We need to ask some searching questions regarding how we approach evangelism in this generation. I suspect that if William Booth were alive in the 1990s, he would be doing things a little differently than he did a century ago. Many Christians have fallen in love with methods and paid too little attention to results. Jesus warned the Pharisees that they were incapable of seeing the new work of God because they were emotionally involved with the old "wineskin," the old way of doing things. We too need to constantly examine our wineskins. Unchecked, we tend to perpetuate ways of sharing the gospel that may actually undermine our message.

LEARNING WHO YOU ARE

Some ill-fitting programs resemble David's efforts to put on Saul's armor when he first headed off to face Goliath. King Saul was trying to help David emerge victorious over Goliath, when

David had a pretty good idea of how to handle the situation nicely. This shepherd had already killed a lion and a bear. The giant, he reasoned, would fall just like those wild animals he'd encountered in the past. David had to use the approach to battling Goliath that suited him rather than listen to eager scriptwriters who wanted to give him half-baked advice on how to take down giants.

Let's be ourselves. Let's give ourselves to God for him to use. In the end that's all we can offer to him. Now that I've stopped trying to be someone I'm not, I've been making some discoveries about who I am. When I aspire to simply be myself, the Holy Spirit's presence is most effectively released through me. My desire isn't to imitate someone else's Christian life, but to be the unique child of God he has created me to be. That discovery has changed the way I communicate the good news to those outside the church.

Sometimes we share the gospel with little verbal explanation. Some of our projects require even little or no direct contact with those we are serving. We have found that these acts of love and service are strong enough to stand on their own without any conversation about God. For example, a woman had parked her car in downtown Cincinnati while she went shopping. One of our teams that feeds parking meters saw that her allotted time was about to expire, put a quarter in the meter, and attached a flyer with our logo at the bottom and this message:

> *While you were gone we fed your parking meter to show you God's love in a practical way. If there is anything further that we can help you with, please call us at 671-0422.*

This woman was so impressed with this deed of kindness that she called an AM radio talk station with the largest audience in this part of the country. She explained to the radio audience what had happened and wondered aloud, "What kind of people would do something like this for others they don't even know?"

The talk-show host followed up by interviewing us over the

phone. At several points he said, "You don't *really* do this stuff, do you? You're kidding me, right?" This man picked up on the fun element in what we were doing. We took him out with us the following Saturday. We had one team giving away coffee in the downtown area, another was washing windshields, still another group went around feeding parking meters. He went along with the group that was cleaning toilets in area restaurants. Every restaurant manager was shocked when we asked if we could clean their toilet for free, no donations accepted. One manager's response was classic: "This sort of thing hasn't been done in hundreds of years. You people are like monks or something."

SEEING THE WORLD
THROUGH JESUS' EYES

After realizing that I had listened more to the scriptwriters than to my own heart, I began to examine my own values. I found it a very helpful exercise to ask myself: "How did Jesus go about his ministry as depicted in Scripture?" I have since made a conscious effort to adopt these values as my own in every area of my life including evangelism. Here are some observations of a script according to Jesus, a man who was the same on the outside as he was on the inside.[2]

Jesus saw through the eyes of the kingdom of God. Like the frontline troops of an army advancing to reclaim lost territory, we are bringing the kingdom of God to bear in this life. Jesus was committed to establishing beachheads in Satan's territory. He was committed to raiding the camps of darkness and setting free the men and women being held captive. As we wait and look for Jesus to come and win the final battle, our primary call is to evangelism.

Jesus saw through the eyes of Scripture. Our desire is to do and teach simply what the Bible says. Its message holds power when it is read and believed just as it is, without imposing any presuppositions and preconceptions onto the text. We must also go beyond knowing the message of the Bible to obeying it.

Jesus saw through the eyes of mercy. Ours is neither to make names for ourselves nor to build lasting institutions, but to meet the needs of broken people through a ministry of mercy. The church is the place where righteousness and mercy meet.

Jesus saw people through the eyes of simplicity. The Son of God did nothing for religious effect. Rather, he operated in a natural, low-key manner.

Jesus saw people through the eyes of integrity. It is vital that what we say is the same as what we do. We must always be careful to speak the truth, deal honestly, and live uprightly.

Jesus saw people through the eyes of his culture. Jesus had the ability to speak the cultural language of his day so that people could understand his message of God's love. We too need to help others see how the gospel can be relevant to their everyday lives.

Jesus saw people through the eyes of reality. Jesus walked in the Spirit and recognized the supernatural works of God. He functioned equally well on a rational plane in his teachings. He both brought and explained the power of the kingdom of God.

Jesus admits the secret of his success: "The Son can do nothing of himself, but what he sees the Father do" (Jn 5:19). If we are to succeed in bringing the good news to those around us, we must place our expectation for success in the right place.

PRESSURE POINTS

For my first five years as a Christian, I mostly spoke the good news but lived out something very different. Later, because of confusion about how to approach evangelism, I moved away from actively sharing my faith. If someone went out of their way to ask me about the Lord I would offer some explanation, but I wasn't obeying the clear call of Scripture to "do the work of an evangelist" (2 Tm 4:5).

I had confused *my* role and *God's* role in the evangelism task. Seeing myself as the evangelist, I saw it as my responsibility to bring people into relationship with Christ. During that first five years, I had approached evangelism as a high-pressure activity—with the majority of the pressure placed on me. Most of the time I was feeling personally guilty for not being more successful. Having created a common double bind, I felt bad about not being more effective in leading others to Christ, but whenever I did try to do evangelism I would take on unbearable responsibility for the outcome. Sheer guilt even motivated me to witness sometimes.

I used to feel that a person's coming to know Christ was a direct result of my efforts. I saw myself as the one delivering others to God's doorstep.

My confusion stemmed from looking to models who were the most gifted, the most mature, the most extroverted members of the Body of Christ. The people who have been effective in evangelism tend to be the ones who write and speak on the subject. These people tend to be strong personalities, sharks as I described them earlier in this chapter.

No matter what our approach to sharing the good news, we will be forced to put pressure on one of these four sources:

1. Pressuring the Christian who is evangelizing
2. Pressuring the person who is being evangelized
3. Pressuring the evangelism program
4. Pressuring God

I believe that most of our evangelistic efforts have falsely put pressure on the first three, while failing to place our trust squarely on God's shoulders where it belongs. We have pressured everything that can be pressured except God. Yet he not only allows us to pressure him, he even invites us. One of my favorite invitations is Jeremiah 33:3, "Call to me, and I will answer you, and show you great and mighty things, which you do not know."

We will never know many things until we begin to see our perpetual lack of wisdom apart from God's intervention in our lives. Zeal for God can be a wondrous weapon if we walk in the attitude Jeremiah suggests. Unfortunately, we often forget the source of all wisdom and strength and attempt to go it alone when we approach evangelism. I used to feel that a person's coming to know Christ was a direct result of my efforts and that I was obligated to get him or her to make that decision. I saw myself as the one delivering others to God's doorstep.

Besides pressuring myself, I was also prone to putting pressure on the program. I was looking for the ultimate outreach plan, one that "really worked" at bringing others to Christ. Almost any approach to doing evangelism will get the attention of Christian leaders because so many of them keep their focus fixed on the program. I don't believe that *any* approach contains the secret for effective evangelism since no program can withstand the pressure of our expectations.

In my attempts to evangelize, I would also put pressure on those hearing the gospel, usually in the form of fear which I swung as an ax over their heads. Many times I would prematurely push people to pray regardless of how they felt or what they understood. Once I had engaged people in a conversation about God, I would always ask them before leaving if they wanted to accept Christ. Many who teach on evangelism present this practice as something positive. I now believe that this is often an inappropriate and untimely question to blurt out to an unprepared stranger. On the many occasions I succeeded in getting a stranger to pray a sinner's prayer with me, I wonder how many did so just to get me off their back.

My sentiments were echoed in a videotaped interview I saw with Fr. Rick Thomas, a Catholic priest from El Paso, Texas. Fr. Rick works with the poor of Juarez, Mexico, just across the border from El Paso. His flock literally lives in the junkyard. As he talked about his ministry to the poor, Fr. Rick said, "We can't *share* the 'good news' and *be* the 'bad news' at the same time. It doesn't work." In a moment of personal soul-searching, I saw that I had communicated God's good news in a bad-news way and probably done more damage than good for the cause of Christ on earth.

> ### "Christians and non-Christians have one thing in common: They both hate evangelism."

If we don't carry the pressure for success in evangelism on our own shoulders, and if we don't place pressure on the hearer or on the program, where should our expectations rest? Where they should have remained from the beginning: on God. Our misplaced expectations will ultimately result in great frustration. In fact, all of our sins and failures can be traced back to our human tendency to find other sources instead of God to meet our needs.

The Westminster Confession states, "The Holy Spirit ... is the only efficient agent in the application of redemption. He regenerates men by his grace, convicts them of sin, moves them to repentance, and persuades and enables them to embrace Jesus Christ by faith. He unites all believers to Christ, dwells in them as their Comforter and Sanctifier, gives them the spirit of Adoption and Prayer, and performs all these gracious offices by which they are sanctified and sealed unto the day of redemption."[3] In short, the Holy Spirit is the only true evangelist who has ever existed. His is the only power in the universe that can turn a convert into a disciple who looks like Jesus Christ. If the Holy Spirit truly is the only evangelist who has ever been, then we are free to remove pressure from the wrong places. We can begin seeing ourselves as coworkers with the Holy Spirit, letting him do what only he can do anyway. Our role is to *enjoy* the flow of God's life through us as we share our joy with others. When we abide in God, we don't just speak or even demonstrate the message of his love, we *embody* that message in a way that makes people stand up and take notice.

When we first approached a local mall for permission to do free gift wrapping at Christmas time, many of the store managers thought we were a bit odd. I went to three interviews during which I was grilled at length about what we were *really* up to. They wanted to know word for word what we were planning to tell people when we wrapped their presents. The primary manager (who happened to be Jewish) was convinced that Christians could do only two things well: take offerings and preach. When we offered to serve with no strings attached, we caught him off guard. Expecting a shark, he didn't know what to do when he caught a dolphin.

Finally the management group agreed to let us wrap gifts, but with the stipulation that if anything unauthorized happened they would close us down without notice. When we passed their tests with flying colors, they raved about the success of the project and invited us to return the following Christmas. We have now wrapped presents for several seasons and received more favor with each passing year from the mall owners. For the past two years they have given us two locations and lots of advertising visibility and even insisted on paying for all the wrapping materials. This past Christmas that amounted to approximately six thousand dollars!

It seems that the fear of the "e" word is universal. Many of us have experienced firsthand the truth of Rebecca Pippert's observation when she says, "Christians and non-Christians have one thing in common: They both hate evangelism."[4] Slowly, as we go about the city giving away both the works and the words of God, we see a growing openness of heart. Christians are becoming bold in an authentic way. Outsiders are wondering why we are showing them so much care. Most importantly, God is building a work force to bring his love to hearts that haven't yet been touched.

Low Risk,
High Grace

*"Our deeds determine us,
as much as we determine our deeds."*
—George Elliot

ONE OF THE DRAWBACKS of doing kindness evangelism in Cincinnati is the weather. We often go through weeks of poor conditions like rain, snow, sleet, severe cold, and tornado watches. The old saying is true, "If you don't like the weather in the Midwest, just wait. It'll change shortly." Many of our initial projects required reasonably sunny weather. After all, who wants their cars washed in the rain!

To deal with the unpredictable climate, we have come up with several all-weather projects. My favorite one is cleaning toilets. Stop and think about it before you reject this idea. Toilets are plentiful—at least one in every home and business. Most of them are in need of at least a little cleaning. And almost anyone can clean a toilet, even someone like me who suffers from a weak stomach. Unpleasant smells, sights, and even noises send me in the opposite direction. When my mom heard I was cleaning toilets for strangers, she commented, *"Steve* is cleaning toilets? That proves there is a God in heaven!"

On a recent ministry outing just before Christmas, we sent several groups into one of the nicer parts of town. Some were cleaning toilets at businesses and restaurants. Our approach is simple and direct. We usually walk up to the person in charge and say, "Hi, we'd like to clean your toilet for free." After they pick themselves up off the floor, they usually say something like, "I could have sworn you just asked me if you could wash my toilet for free, but I know that can't be true. No one has ever cleaned our toilet for free."

On this particular day, a Christmas party was in progress at a well-known restaurant and bar. They seemed to be having a good time eating, drinking, and carrying on. While one of our teams was working in the restroom, a doctor came in who had been drinking a bit too much. When he asked why they were there, they explained themselves. This man told them he too was a Christian but was unfortunately in a compromising position that day. It wasn't long before he asked the team to pray for him— right there in the men's restroom! They reported that the doctor did most of the praying, asking God to touch his life and renew him in his Christian walk. I would like to have been a mouse in the corner listening to this man explain to his wife later how his Christmas party went!

This story illustrates one of the primary benefits of servant evangelism: it combines *low risk* with *high grace*. Every ministry venture involves an aspect of both risk and grace. In order to be successful, we must live within the limits of our emotional, financial, spiritual, and relational budget, so to speak. As I see it, very few church leaders have a good grasp on the cost of projects before they leap in with both feet. If secular businesses operated that way, most of them would have gone bankrupt long ago. Let's examine how these factors of risk and grace affect the area of evangelism.

THE RISK FACTOR

Jesus referred to the risk element of the kingdom of God in this parable: "What king, going to make war against another king, does not sit down first and consider whether he is able with ten thousand to meet him who comes against him with twenty thousand? Or else, while the other is still a great way off, he sends a delegation and asks for conditions of peace" (Lk 14:31-32). Jesus evidently considered this king wise for counting the cost before venturing into battle.

Many attempts to share the good news rate high on obedience and enthusiasm but low on careful consideration of what we may be getting ourselves into.

Every outreach carries a price tag, whether that cost is readily evident or more hidden. Some costs are easy to measure; some aren't. Many attempts to share the good news rate high on obedience and enthusiasm but low on careful consideration of what we may be getting ourselves into. What are some of the risks involved in bringing the good news to those who need to hear it?

Relational risk. First, we must consider the relational risk. Let's say that I step out as a leader and tell others that we're going to have "big fun" by knocking on doors. Take it from a veteran door-knocker: the average Christian will have anything *but* fun. If I gather and train an evangelism group from my church with this kind of promise, I will have eroded my credibility as a leader. I would be guilty of underestimating the relational risk of that particular outreach. The next time I invite these same people out to have "fun," they will all think twice about whether or not they can stand that much fun in a single morning.

Financial risk. Some evangelistic approaches are very expensive. Not long ago a large crusade was held in Cincinnati with a number of positive results. Numerous churches which didn't normally associate with one another came together in unity. Many lay people were trained and encouraged in their personal evangelism techniques. And many people came forward and made a profession of faith, in addition to those who made a decision to rededicate their lives to the Lord.

But by the time the choir had finished singing the last hymn and the evangelist had packed his bags for home, the downside of this outreach became evident: the enormous cost. For a week-long crusade, the total price tag amounted to well over one million dollars! I myself received letters for nearly a year soliciting funds to cover the remainder of the debt. I think all the churches that participated in this crusade were pleased with the results, but I don't believe anyone realized how much hard work would be involved in paying off the bills. Perhaps the organizers would have thought twice if they had literally counted the cost of the crusade beforehand.

Emotional risk. The emotional risk is probably the greatest cost to consider. As a borderline introvert, I personally need to do projects that don't require a lot of interaction with strangers. Going door to door is a traumatic experience for most people because of the enormous rejection rate. One friend recently confided in me that he was often so afraid of being rejected that he would pray that no one would be home when he went door-knocking in his efforts to start a new church. He would sometimes have to just stop for the day because he could take no more dissenting voices. And this man is the gifted pastor of a nationally-known church. If this experienced minister struggled with talking to total strangers, what does the average Christian do? Yet, the most popular approaches to bringing the good news require huge emotional risks.

At one time I regularly went out with a Christian group which is well-known for its confrontational style of street witnessing. The first time I went out with them, they gave me a police whistle along with a pile of tracts. "So what's the whistle for?" I innocently asked.

"Sometimes people get pretty mad at us for giving out tracts and talking on the streets. Every once in a while one of us gets attacked. If you do, just blow the whistle and we'll know you're in trouble and come running."

Now that's how I spell R-I-S-K.

Spiritual risk. Lastly, evangelism entails a spiritual risk. Whenever we seek to win someone to Christ, we raise the ire of the Evil One. Satan is not one bit happy when people escape his grasp and start following Jesus. Carriers of the good news become, to some degree, walking targets of the enemy. The spiritual reality behind our practical efforts must be prayerfully taken into account when we aspire to do evangelism.

In light of all these risks, it's no wonder the word "evangelism" so often instills fear in us. Unfortunately, our leaders have done much to perpetuate this fear by not balancing the risk with the available assets. If we hope to present a picture of evangelism attainable by the average Christian, we'll have to rediscover the grace of God to meet the risk.

THE GRACE FACTOR

It's one thing for people to show up to do evangelism, but is the Lord also going to show up when we arrive? Scripture assures us that God is present with the believer wherever he or she goes. We have his *abiding* presence, but I have experienced a *ministry* presence of the Holy Spirit that seems to ebb and flow.

Matthew made reference to this reality in describing Jesus' visit to his hometown of Nazareth: "He did not do many mighty works there because of their unbelief" (Mt 13:58). As one who has shown up to do ministry when the Lord stayed home, I can assure you that it's no fun being out there without the immediate presence of the Holy Spirit. If we take an honest look at the typical evangelistic efforts being used in most of our churches, we can see that many of them actually require very little of God's active blessing in order for the program to keep rolling forward. Such attempts at sharing the good news will inevitably prove ineffective in the long run.

It's one thing for people to show up to do evangelism, but is the Lord also going to show up when we arrive?

♦♦♦

As the Son of God, Jesus had high expectations for God's ministering presence to be upon his every move through life. I believe God still heals, but many pastors believe differently. One of their primary objections to the healing ministry comes in the form of a question: "If God still heals, then why don't you just go down to the hospital and begin praying for cancer patients from bed to bed?"

I receive that question as coming from a sincere heart, but anyone asking it doesn't understand that the ministering presence of God does not remain at the same level each time we pray. And it wasn't that way for Jesus either, as pointed out in the Matthew 13 verse. So why did Jesus see so many people healed when he prayed for the sick? The answer lies in the fifth chapter of John, which describes how Jesus healed a man at the pool of Bethesda who had been ill for thirty-eight years. How did he pick out this one man from a "multitude of invalids, blind, lame, and paralyzed"? All of them needed healing, but the Lord touched only one that day. Jesus explained: "Most assuredly, I say to you, the Son can do nothing of himself, but *what he sees the Father do;* for whatever he does, the Son also does in like manner" (Jn 5:19).

Jesus experienced an enormous success rate in praying for the sick because he prayed only for those he saw the Father touching and healing. The Son pursued only the "high grace" cases, the ones the Father pointed out. Praying for the sick simply meant *noticing* the ones the Father was already touching, then *identifying* that touch, and *blessing* it to be done.

Successfully bringing the good news to others requires involving ourselves in projects that require the presence of the Lord. Our motto must be, "If God shows up everything is going to be fine. If he doesn't show up, nothing much is going to happen here." I have a pastor friend in the Baltimore area who has learned to walk in that mindset. He felt for some time that God wanted his church to become involved in outreach at the local high school. When he approached the school on a number of occasions to ask permission, those in charge graciously replied, "You know, we just can't mix church and state. We can't officially allow you on campus. Sorry."

About a year ago this pastor relayed his frustrations to me in a conversation. I suggested that he consider doing an outreach off campus, but still close enough to touch significant numbers of students in short spaces of time. A few weeks later he pulled off his first outreach—a flaming success! About a dozen folks from his church set up a folding table at a corner near the high school and offered the passing students a free soft drink.

Over the following weeks this same team gave away popsicles, cassette tapes with Christian music, and buttons with the slogan "I love you—J.C." Before long this church was touching three to four hundred students at a youth meeting every Friday evening. My friend later related this story to me and said, "You know, it's amazing what a can of Coke along with God's presence can do. It can open a human heart to God's love!"

CHOOSE YOUR QUADRANT

The elements of risk and grace suggest a variety of possible combinations in reaching out to others. Some of the choices are livable only for "Super Hero" Christians. Others are workable for your basic chicken who loves the Lord. It is important that you find the quadrant that fits you best.

Low Risk Low Grace	High Risk Low Grace
High Risk **High Grace**	**Low Risk** **High Grace**

Risk – What is the cost emotionally?
  spiritually?
  relationally?
  financially?
Grace – How much of God's presence is necessary for this outreach to be a success?

Low risk–low grace. Low-risk evangelism may be attainable by the average Christian, but I don't want to ever be involved in an outreach project that doesn't require God's presence in order to succeed. One popular approach in starting a new church involves randomly calling large numbers of people and inviting them to attend. While that program has been successful on occasion, I have heard far more failure stories. There's not much risk involved for the person making the phone calls, but there's not much supernatural working of the Spirit of God either. This past year I have received several of these phone calls myself. In the most recent invitation to attend a new church in Cincinnati, the person was calling from Michigan!

Some might say, "Some outreach is better than no outreach." Perhaps so, but I feel that if God is not clearly present in our projects, then we are wasting our time by essentially trying to flog a dead horse. Jesus promised that we could do nothing without him, but with him we would bear much fruit, fruit that would remain (Jn 15:5, 16). As we hunger for a greater measure of his presence and grace, we are assured that we will bear much fruit in sharing the good news of God's love.

High risk–low grace. A popular television comedy from the sixties, *Hogan's Heroes,* repeated a common phrase in nearly every episode. If Sergeant Schultz messed up one more time, his superiors threatened to send him to the dreaded "Russian Front," an actual place where the warfare was so intense that very few came back unwounded. Unfortunately, a lot of the outreach projects I have been involved with over the years fall into this "Russian-front" category.

Unfortunately, a lot of the outreach projects
I have been involved with over the years fall into
this "Russian-front" category.

Of the four possibilities, the high risk–low grace quadrant is most likely to discourage people from doing evangelism if they continue in that vein for long. These kinds of outreaches also cause the outside community to label Christians as fanatics. In short, we're talking about an approach that is costly and will not yield much return. That sounds like the description of a couple of cars I've owned!

On numerous occasions I have gone with groups knocking on

doors to share the gospel. This approach is high risk because we are invading the private space of people, that special place called home. Fifty years ago, when most Americans lived on farms, people might have welcomed such visitors, but not anymore. This approach is low grace because it puts the primary pressure for results on the person sharing the gospel.

Door-to-door evangelism usually entails explaining the gospel and then systematically answering someone's questions. The belief is that if we can adequately answer their questions and objections, then they will logically come to the Lord. In this approach, the person with the quickest mind and the best grasp of language skills usually makes the best evangelist.

My own experimentation with a number of approaches to evangelism has indicated that they all work to one degree or another. The one exception to that rule has been the survey method. Perhaps you yourself have been surveyed at the mall or in the parking lot of a sporting event. This approach disguises the evangelist as a research interviewer who requests information in order to put the interviewee at ease. The survey starts with simple, safe questions.

First we ask, "How long have you lived in this community?"

We move on to, "Do you like living in this community?"

Then we touch on personal tastes, "Is your car American-made or an import?"

Finally, we move in for the kill with, "Would you say you have a personal relationship with Jesus Christ or not?"

Christian researcher George Barna has awarded the survey approach with the Millstone Award in special recognition for a ministry practice that impedes the gospel in America.[1] Clearly this approach is deceptive. We gain the trust of those we're interviewing and then—BAM!—we spring it on them. Just when they were getting relaxed in the conversation, the Christian trying to share the good news shows that people who love Jesus are not to be trusted and in fact may be out-and-out hypocrites.

Earlier in my Christian life I participated in a long string of high risk–low grace outreaches. I guess I had a high capacity for

failure. For example, I attempted several evangelistic Bible studies during college. I'm fairly good at talking people into things
they aren't interested in doing, but this approach challenged
even my sales skills. The idea behind this approach is to invite several nonbelievers to your dorm room for an hour of Bible study.
The study of God's Word is always powerful and worthwhile, but
getting people to attend is a difficult trick to pull off.

I believe high-risk approaches to sharing the good news can be
effective in certain settings. I liken sharing the good news to playing
golf. The rules of this game allow thirteen different clubs to be carried in the golf bag, each one appropriate at some point in the
game. At the beginning of each hole, the goal is to drive the ball as
far as possible down the fairway. For that shot a wood club is appropriate. Getting the ball on the green usually requires an iron club. A
putter is best for the final goal of sinking the ball into the cup.

Imagine a golfer making the claim, "I'm committed to just
using my putter. I'm a putting specialist. I have a whale of a time
getting from the tee to the green, but once I'm within fifty feet
of the cup, watch out—I'm deadly!" It would be equally ridiculous to think of a golfer using only a wood for his entire game.

Evangelism works the same way. We need an entire "golf bag"
full of approaches for reaching those in our communities. Though
many of the traditional approaches to sharing the gospel are rather
high risk, they have proven to be effective over the years. We
would be committing an error in judgment to drop every other
approach to evangelism just to adopt servant evangelism. I vigor-
ously support any approach that effectively encounters the
unchurched. My hope is that we can grow in our effectiveness by
growing in our diversity, that we can learn how to draw on the
appropriate "club" at the right time in bringing the good news.

I believe high-risk approaches are particularly effective in the
final phases of the evangelism process where people are making a
personal commitment to follow Jesus. These same methods often
come up short when we focus on them to the exclusion of others.
When we have only one means for sharing the good news, we
will surely limit our effectiveness in evangelism.

High risk–high grace. Ventures in this category include "power evangelism," foreign missions, and starting a new church, all of which center around the direct confrontation of God's kingdom and the kingdom of the Evil One.

The term "power encounter" aptly describes the spiritual warfare that takes place when God's presence collides with the powers of darkness in the lives of the lost. The manifest presence of the Lord and powerful gifts of the Holy Spirit convince unbelievers of the reality of God. Such ministries are exciting and make for goose-pimple stories, but they are not for the faint of heart. Each of these approaches carries a high requirement for God's presence in order to succeed.

Power evangelism begins when God sovereignly releases his power by giving someone supernatural insight into another person's life. This approach is a bit tricky, first because we cannot manufacture those insights from the Lord. Only God can initiate prophetic encounters. I believe God desires to speak in these ways, but my experience is that he doesn't do so with great regularity.

Second, every human being remains subject to error even when the Lord does speak. After moving in the gifts of the Spirit for years now, I still proceed with great caution when I sense the Lord has shown me something about another person. I am acutely aware of the possibility of my being mistaken. My opening words are usually, "I may be wrong, but I think the Lord is saying this...." I am a frail human who has tens of thousands of thoughts going through my head every day, only a few of which are inspired by the Lord.

The high-risk element of power evangelism is obvious. It takes tremendous courage to walk up to a total stranger and tell him or her what you sense the Lord is saying. In fact, it takes more courage than most pastors have, not to mention the members of the flock following their leadership. When I first began hearing from the Lord in this way, I thought the day would soon come when most of my church would be experiencing a significant level of spiritual gifting. I thought it would be commonplace to hear dynamic healing stories. I was wrong. I naively thought the average Christian would be more courageous than I have found to be the case.

Having something to *give* seems to open the door for significant conversation. Fear on both sides is diminished once we enter into an encounter with a simple deed of kindness. These acts give us the baby steps we need to gradually walk into others' lives. With each step a little more courage seems to come our way and we grow steadily in our ability to interact with nonbelievers. When a divine appointment is set up by the Lord and we happen to be his spokesperson, we need lots of courage to step out and be bold.

Fear on both sides is diminished once we enter into an encounter with a simple deed of kindness.

We have noticed that as we are serving others, we sometimes become aware of a current difficulty they may be facing—a sort of spiritual sensitivity from the Lord. One morning we were going door to door in a middle-class, black neighborhood on the north side of Cincinnati offering to wash the windshields of the cars parked in the driveways. The people of this neighborhood had always been receptive to us, if not a little amazed at the notion of white men going door to door in a predominantly black area. This particular Saturday, Dan, a new believer and member of our church, was with me.

We came to a house where a woman was talking on a princess-style phone with a long extension cord. She put the phone down momentarily after we rang the doorbell and asked what we wanted. We explained our project and got busy cleaning the three cars in her driveway. As we were finishing up, the conversation between Dan and me shifted from the current state of Reds baseball, to politics, to—out of nowhere—the clear sense that this woman had recently been divorced and was barely hanging on to her sanity.

My first thought was, *Boy, am I a judgmental person! Why am I thinking these thoughts about this nice lady?* A moment later, God showed me further that this woman had two teenage children who were giving her fits. I sensed that the combination of her ex-husband and children was driving her to the edge of her ability to cope, but that God wanted to touch her in power.

It's one thing to have a sense that you may be *getting* something from the Lord, and a completely different challenge to actually *share* what you think the Lord is saying. The words we receive will carry an impact only if we use great wisdom in knowing how to share that spiritual insight. In this case I was operating more in faith than in great confidence. My heart began to thump loudly and I felt a little dizzy. With little polish I went to the door and knocked. When the woman put her hand over the phone and thanked us for washing her windshields, I boldly stepped out on a limb and asked her, "By the way, have you recently been divorced and are your kids driving you crazy?"

The woman's reaction to my question was amazing. She immediately burst into tears and hung up the phone. If we devised a scale for rating tears—with a level one being a slight trickle and a level five being weepy, this woman was sobbing at a level nine. Her tears were leaping out horizontally!

My friend Dan didn't know what to think. I didn't know what to think. I certainly didn't expect this sort of reaction to my question. We both felt a little embarrassed at this encounter. All we could think to pray was for God's mercy to come to this lady. After a few minutes the shaking and weeping gradually subsided. Betty, as we found her name was, then asked how we knew about her situation. "I don't know anything about your situation. The Lord just spoke to me as I was washing your windshield."

On another occasion I took a group out in Birmingham, Alabama, to wash windshields at a shopping center parking lot. One woman, who had expressed fear of going out with the group, was washing the windshield of an empty car. As she did she noticed an infant carseat and had a strong impression that the baby who sat in that carseat had recently been very ill. She felt so moved that she prayed a simple prayer for the baby, just in case her sense was correct.

Just as she finished washing the windshield, a woman approached the car with a grocery cart. This woman expressed thankfulness for the clean windshield and began to load her groceries into the trunk. The woman from our church had a clear sense that she ought to offer to pray for the baby. Mustering all the courage she could find, she blurted out, "Has the baby that sits in that carseat been deathly ill lately?"

With that the mother burst out weeping, saying, "Yes, my baby almost died recently. How do you know so much about my baby?" The woman who had timidly stepped out to wash windshields got much more than she bargained for: instruction as to the proper use of a squeegee as well as a word of knowledge that opened the heart of a stranger struggling with pain and fear.

When power encounters do happen, they make our job as bringers of God's love incredibly easier. The drawback is that none of us can cause a prophetic insight from God to come to us. I can't cause anyone to be healed or touched by the presence of God. My only hope is that God in his sovereignty will come and touch the needy, and hopefully allow me to be a part of that encounter.

We have seen a lot of healings over the years, but they seem to come in spurts. I don't know why, but we seem to go through seasons when these encounters are common, and then long stretches when they almost don't happen at all. As far as I can tell, our hearts are equally open from meeting to meeting, but the evidence of God's power in our midst seems to be ever changing.

In some ways I see power encounters and servant evangelism as "kissing cousins." They both work on the basis of disarming a stranger by demonstrating God's immediate presence. The person is enabled to see the power of God—whether that be accomplished by a free Coke or a word of knowledge that reveals hidden thoughts and emotions. Both acts can be equally powerful in demonstrating God's love. But beyond that common element of making an entry point by showing God's immediate presence, the two approaches diverge greatly. Receiving words of knowledge when doing kindness evangelism remains the exception in our experience.

Low risk-high grace. I believe that this is the best area for most Christians to explore in reaching out to others with the good news. Servant evangelism is low risk in that it doesn't require a lot of money, time, expertise, or emotional energy to be effective. It is high grace because we carry out this ministry with simple honesty toward God. "God, if you are upon this project, something of significance will happen. But, Lord, this is just a simple service we're performing. We know that nothing of lasting value will be imparted here unless you are upon us."

More traditional high-risk approaches ask people to do more in evangelism than they are capable of doing. We have, in a sense, set the high jump bar at seven feet, a height that only Olympic-level athletes can clear. Expectations for results have been set at an impossible emotional height for most Christians. One look at the task and most of us shake our heads. I know I could never pole vault seven feet. My only hope for looking good would be to cheat and use a hidden trampoline for extra oomph!

After a while, the consistent theme of rejection and failure overwhelms the average Christian. Eventually, most of us just throw up our arms in frustration and quit. We become carp: sitting on the bottom of the river and sucking mud, but at least we're safe. We become victims of a faulty conclusion that says, "There must be something wrong with me and my walk with the Lord because I really don't enjoy doing evangelism."

No matter how many clever ways we use to prop up our approach to evangelism—"new and improved" programs, videos, books, and seminars—nothing much is going to change until we alter the basic proposition. Unless we can lower the risk and raise the sense of God's presence in our encounters, the average Christian will continue to see evangelism as something only experts can do. Thank God for the experts, but I don't think that's what God intends. Evangelism doesn't have to be that way. I have been learning to walk free from the sense of guilt and fear in evangelism by minimizing the risk and maximizing the need for God's grace. Low risk and high grace fit together nicely.

Eventually, most of us just throw up our arms in frustration and quit. We become carp: sitting on the bottom of the river and sucking mud, but at least we're safe.

◆◆◆

FROM PRAGUE TO FORT WORTH

I spoke one summer at a gathering of several dozen churches in Prague. I was slated to speak twice, once to a smaller gathering of pastors and later to the entire group of several thousand. After speaking to the pastors there was a lot of discussion as to whether they felt good about my presenting this approach to evangelism to the larger group. The leaders weren't sure they agreed with the approach I described. With some reluctance, they agreed to have me share with the larger crowd. Afterward I invited any interested people to come out the following morning to do a few kindness evangelism projects.

I was only prepared for a dozen or so, but to my surprise, a couple of hundred people showed up! When I saw the number of participants I sent someone to the store to buy chewing gum. Gum is inexpensive there, so for about fifty dollars we were able to buy several thousand sticks. For several hours we had gum teams going about the streets of downtown Prague. We had also purchased in advance enough windshield washing tools to equip several teams.

When the group regathered to share their experience, I sensed enormous excitement in the air. They were excited because, in the words of one man, "this is something anyone can do." As the stories of that day trickled in over the next few weeks, the leadership group grew more and more excited. I was invited back to speak another summer to a conference of two thousand. The leaders want to take all of the attendees out into the city and do outreaches at forty or so locations around Prague.

While speaking at a Bible school in Fort Worth, I commented that low risk–high grace outreach succeeds easily. For the most part, the group was made up of veteran Christians who had long ago grown accustomed to high-risk evangelism and ceased seeing new opportunities for carrying the good news to the world. They had gotten used to an insurmountable high-jump bar and thought that's just the way evangelism happened to be.

I challenged those gathered by asking how many of them had recently interacted with someone outside the church. I was not surprised to find that only 1 or 2 percent of them responded in the affirmative. This group, like many veteran Christians, had created an unrealistic image of evangelism. That high risk–low grace picture caused them to live in a very confined universe that was nearly 100 percent full of just Christians.

I challenged this group to find new ways of experimenting with lower risk approaches to getting out of the church and into the community. With a marker in my hand we brainstormed for a few minutes. Being unfamiliar with the area, I didn't know what we could spontaneously do in that part of town. After a few minutes of discussion we decided to go to a laundromat located just one hundred feet from the front door of the school, where we would put quarters into the washing machines for customers as they walked in.

The students asked me what the proper technique for doing this was. I told them just to watch me. Little did they know that I had never done a laundromat outreach—I was figuring out how to do this as I went along! With several students peering over my shoulder, a mother with two kids in tow walked in with

a huge pile of laundry. When I saw which machine she was planning to use, I put quarters in the machine and simply asked, "Do
you want hot or cold water?" She answered with a little surprise
in her voice, "Cold. Why do you ask?"

"We're a group of Christians doing a community service
project to show God's love in a practical way. We want to pay for
your wash this morning just to demonstrate God's love to you."

As you might imagine, this lady had lots of questions. I asked
one of the female students to answer her questions and help her
fold laundry. Thirty minutes later I left the laundromat. All
around the place the students were connecting with the people
who had come in to wash their clothes. Some were engrossed in
conversation, others were laughing and telling stories. The first
woman we helped was quietly praying and weeping with the girl
who had stepped out to help her.

When I spoke again at the school the next day, I opened by
asking the students who had gone to the laundromat to share
their perceptions. One young guy began to tell what happened
and broke down crying. He said, "I saw God really touch lives
yesterday. And to think that in just a few minutes we were able to
get into their lives, just by feeding some quarters in the washing
machines. I never thought it could be this easy bringing God's
love to people."

THE DISCIPLES STARTED WITH
LOW RISKS TOO

In his three-year ministry Jesus spent most of the early days
with the disciples showing them how to do what he did. From
the early pages of the gospel accounts, we see Jesus actively taking risks. He was casting out demons, preaching the message that
the kingdom of God was at hand, miraculously feeding large
numbers of people, even raising the dead on occasion.

Most of the three years Jesus was with the twelve, the action
revolved around him. Then gradually, step by manageable step,

he imparted ministry opportunity to the apostles. When he fed the four thousand (Mt 15:32-38), the disciples' job was to carry the bread and fish from Jesus to the people. Afterwards they picked up the mess. That was a manageable risk. Later these men were sent out for just a few days to do some of what they had been watching Jesus do. They too cast out demons, healed, cared for and fed others, and preached the arrival of God's kingdom (Lk 9:1-6). It wasn't until much later, after Jesus had returned to the Father, that the disciples began to do apostolic works similar to those done by Jesus.

The kingdom of God is sown in the hearts of growing and maturing disciples bit by bit, manageable risk by manageable risk. Of course, all of us can tell a story or two about having to step out of our comfort zones occasionally in order to make progress in our Christian lives, but generally we need to proceed at a more conservative pace. We need to first learn how to jump an attainable height before we move on to the next slightly increased level.

We don't have to have all *of the answers a non-Christian might ask in order to make a significant impact.*

The Christian life is meant to be simple rather than complicated. One does not need to be a mature believer to perform acts of kindness. In fact, a brand-new believer can effectively do this sort of evangelism. We don't have to have *all* of the answers a non-Christian might ask in order to make a significant impact.

On the Friday evening before Labor Day, rush hour traffic was backed up for nearly a mile at the corner where our church is located. The temperature was ninety-five degrees with a matching humidity level. About ten of us from the church quickly went into action to touch several hundred hot, frustrated motorists with God's love. We iced down four hundred soft drinks and set up signs just down the road: "Free Drinks Ahead."

As the drivers approached the stop sign, we would ask, "Would you like diet or regular?"

"Diet or regular what?" came the skeptical reply.

"We're giving away free soft drinks to show people God's love in a practical way."

"But why?"

"Just because God loves you."

Reactions varied greatly. Some people smiled, some shook their heads, several mouths dropped open. Most were a little stunned to receive something for free. A United Parcel Service driver drove away saying, "But I don't even know you guys. Why would you do something like this for me?"

In less than an hour we had given out all four hundred cokes. We had spoken with about six hundred people (some didn't take a coke but wondered what we were doing), and we even made the local radio station's helicopter traffic report. While we were cleaning up afterward one man commented, "This was so much fun I don't know if it even counts as 'evangelism.'" Another guy standing nearby responded, "I don't know if it is evangelism, but it'll do until the real thing comes along! Whatever we did, a lot of people experienced the reality and love of God this afternoon."

Just as with the apostles, Jesus is patient with our growth. He knows that most of those who represent him and his kingdom will be around for a long time to come. Perhaps some of us will be singled out to participate in special high risk–high grace activities, but I believe most Christians are meant to dwell in the realm of low risk–high grace. Regardless of our quadrant, God is intent on our reaching a place of maturity in his kingdom where we will be consistently carrying his life to a world that is dying for lack of his presence and love.

BEYOND US
AND THEM

*"Man stand for long time with mouth open
before roast duck fly in."*
—Chinese Proverb

I MAGINE GOING THROUGH several days at a parachute training school where the teachers had covered every phase of successful jumping. The students learned how to select the right parachute and how to pack them, even the importance of color coordinating one's jumping apparel. They had studied great parachutists of the past, read accident statistics of those who had failed, and then simulated jumps. Finally, the training ended, the tests were graded, and a graduation ceremony was held to acknowledge all those who had passed.

As the president of the school spoke about its long and proud heritage, everyone was happy—except one student. Although it was out of place right in the middle of their celebration, he raised his hand. When the speaker asked what was wrong, this one student meekly stood up and said, "I feel silly getting a certificate showing that I'm qualified to parachute. I haven't actually jumped out of an airplane yet."

With that everyone in the room turned, gasped simultaneously, and sternly replied, "Don't you know, we don't *parachute* anymore. We just study and talk about parachuting!"

I have experienced much the same attitude in being trained to do evangelism. As a student at a fine Bible school in the Los Angeles area in the mid-seventies, I joined many other young people from unchurched backgrounds. We had all experienced profound conversions to Christ in and around the Jesus Movement which was then flourishing in Southern California. The students, who were new to Christ and placed little value in church-related traditions, combined with the faculty members who had known Christ most of their lives made for a combustible mixture.

In this fertile environment I soon became involved in the "evangelism team," a group of about a dozen people who met for three hours every Friday evening to do evangelism. Early in the school year we all experienced great enthusiasm for going out to share God's love with nonbelievers. Even so, it seemed only appropriate that we first adequately prepare before venturing out. We read several books on the topic, saw some films, had lively discussions about how we could most effectively evangelize. We even did role-playing as a way to practice sharing our faith.

Eventually Christmas vacation hit and we hadn't yet finished our training time. School resumed and—you know how time passes quickly—before we knew it, spring break was upon us. About the first of May it dawned on me: the "evangelism team" should have been called the "preparation team." We really didn't do any evangelism. What we really did was talk, pray, and train for evangelism. Our group never did go out into the community that year.

One Friday evening toward the end of the year, I made that observation to the leader of the team. He patiently responded in a patronizing way, "Steve, I love your enthusiasm, but we just aren't ready to go out yet. When you get older in the Lord, you'll see the wisdom in what we have done this year." I was being told that later, when I grew more mature in Christ, it would make sense that the "evangelism team" really didn't do evangelism. I didn't get it then, and I still don't get it.

I operated as a sort of Christian agoraphobic: loving the Lord, but afraid to go outside the house of the Lord.

♦♦♦

I've spent most of my Christian life being stuck in these kinds of fears and myths about life. I operated as a sort of Christian agoraphobic: loving the Lord, but afraid to go outside the house of the Lord. In recent years, however, I've been venturing out of the Christian ghetto which once kept me bound. I've been saying no to the fears and myths that once gripped me and kept me in a place of inactivity. To put it another way, I've been daring to color outside of the lines.

THE KINGDOM: THEORETICAL OR PRACTICAL?

We gear our Wednesday night services mostly toward believers so that we can spend a longer time in worship and encourage the practice of the gifts of the Spirit. I began to notice a man who usually attended. It's hard *not* to notice Willy. He is six feet five inches tall, has a blond mohawk, and dozens of tattoos covering both arms. His most evident tattoo is a frog imprinted on the side of his head. Whenever I'm near Willy, the eyes of this frog seem to be looking at me no matter where I stand. When I first questioned Willy about his regular attendance at our meetings, he responded, "I can feel something here so I come and listen to the songs you sing."

Recently Willy showed me that he had been featured in *Tattoo* magazine. Until then, I didn't even know such a magazine existed. When I asked him what he did for a living, Willy answered, "I buy and sell things." My sense was that it just wouldn't be appropriate to ask him exactly *what* he bought and sold.

I've been trying to build bridges with this guy even though we're from incredibly different worlds. I don't have a single tattoo and I wear polo shirts and khaki pants. Maybe I hadn't made a lasting impression on this man. Nevertheless, I felt good about trying to step out of my comfort zone and into a very different life circle to show God's love to Willy.

Like the parachuting school, it seems we don't *do* evangelism so much as we talk about it. For the most part we are satisfied just studying the good news. A multitude of fears and myths regarding *us* as Christians and *them* as non-Christians often keeps us from sharing the gospel with those in our community. I must admit that I was afraid of Willy. My friends in Bible school were afraid of reaching out. Fear seems to be a cruel theme in our lives, one that keeps us from doing what God has called us to do.

Jesus tells a story of three men who were stuck in the same kind of fears (Lk 10:25-37). While two of them continued in their fears, one made a bold escape. Jesus was asked by a lawyer in the crowd, "What shall I do to inherit eternal life?"

Jesus' answer was essentially, "It's very practical. Love God and love your fellow man."

The man, wanting to minimize his level of responsibility, asked, "Who is my neighbor?" Jesus replied with the parable of the good Samaritan:

"A certain man went down from Jerusalem to Jericho, and fell among thieves, who stripped him of his clothing, wounded him, and departed, leaving him half dead. Now by chance a certain priest came down that road. And when he saw him, he passed by on the other side. Likewise a Levite, when he arrived at the place, came and looked, and passed by on the other side. But a certain Samaritan, as he journeyed, came where he was.

And when he saw him, he had compassion on him, and went to him and bandaged his wounds, pouring on oil and wine; and he set him on his own animal, brought him to an inn, and took care of him. On the next day, when he departed, he took out two denarii, gave them to the innkeeper, and said to him, 'Take care of him; and whatever more you spend, when I come again, I will repay you.'"

Jesus then asked the lawyer, "Which of these three do you think proved to be a neighbor to the man who fell into the robbers' hands?"

The lawyer replied, "The one who showed mercy toward him."

And Jesus said to him, "Go and do the same." Jesus' answer to the question "Who is my neighbor?" was in brief, "Your neighbor is the person right in front of you with a need in his or her life." No matter what those people look like, even if they happen to be our natural enemies, we are called to show them the love of God.

In other words, the way we (the Church) treat them (the unchurched) serves as a litmus test of our spiritual health.

Jesus tells us that the way we treat others displays the condition of our hearts. In other words, the way *we* (the Church) treat *them* (the unchurched) serves as a litmus test of our spiritual health. The three men in the parable were offered the same test: What to do about a man beaten to the point of death and left lying in a ditch? None of them were aware at the time that they were taking a test; only one passed by responding to the need placed in his path.

Frankly, most of my Christian life has resembled the actions and attitudes of the priest and the Levite who walked right past the wounded man. Let's take a closer look at these two men who had separated themselves from the world, people who were held in a vise by the same fears that affect you and me.

The priest and the Levite saw God's kingdom as a *separate* kingdom. They saw the law of the temple as being above any human consideration. The life of the priest centered on his pre-scribed temple duties at weekly services such as reading from the Torah, making sacrifices, and preaching. His role at the temple meant more to him than the pain of the man lying at his feet.

This first man was likely on a priestly mission, perhaps on his way to perform his temple duties that very day. No doubt, he remembered the law saying that a man who touched a dead body was unclean for seven days (Nm 19:11). The priest might have been afraid that the wounded man was dead and refused to risk being made unclean. In his attempt to be holy, he had discon-nected himself from the hurting world around him, the wounded whom God loves.

The priest's separation from the world made sense according to his narrow religious sphere, but it made no sense to the broader world. In the eyes of those outside the Jewish religion, he had valued ritual and ceremony more than human life. The priest could only function in his comfort zone, the temple. Outside of that setting, he was like a horse wearing blinders.

The Levite also lived in a reality of his own making, one that was just as false as the priest's. This man saw God's kingdom as a place where the ultimate goal centered around being correct and holding to the right knowledge of God. As a legal expert in Jewish law, the Levite occupied himself with theories and specu-lations. He perceived power as flowing from doing things right. To him life was an equation, and he was God's answer man. The only problem was, no one outside of his circle was asking the kinds of questions the Levite could answer.

The goal of most churchgoers is to be free from pain, a reality which all of us will experience to one degree or another until the day we die. Old pains are being healed by the Lord's presence and power in our lives, but plenty of new ones keep coming along. We're all trying to forget the personal pain that can either keep us frozen away from the mainstream of the Lord's activity or else open doors into the broader community.

The personal pain of the priest and Levite kept them away from life and focused on their own fears and myths. I'm learning not to allow my pain to keep me paralyzed and sequestered from the world around me which is the object of God's love. Each time I step out of the arena of the church world and into the world of the unchurched, I find that a little bit more of God's healing comes to me.

True kingdom vision will always be people-centered. The priest and Levite were inwardly centered, caught up in the rules and activities of their religious system. They were in a hurry because they had programs to run. Their programs appeared altogether worthwhile, even biblical and obedient, but these two men were ultimately corrupt because they didn't see people as being at the center of God's kingdom.

INTOLERANCE IS NOT HOLINESS

Scripture required those who served in the temple to be people who lived righteous lives. The priest and Levite no doubt sought personal holiness, a necessary aspiration for all who would follow the Lord. But what these men displayed was not holiness but a counterfeit version which became apparent when they walked past the man lying in the ditch. The priest and Levite were actually seeking to please people rather than God.

When speaking at a church some time ago, I mentioned that sometimes I watch TV and go to the movies. I enjoy going to the movies, I explained, because it is relaxing and serves as a good break from the intensity of my schedule. Later in my talk I gave an illustration from a popular movie which had been filmed in that state, a movie which Christians would have little difficulty endorsing. When I asked who had seen this film, only two people out of a crowd of over two hundred admitted to having done so. The pastor of the church later told me that he personally knew of many members of his congregation who had in fact seen this movie, but they were unwilling to admit it among their friends!

Often what Christians think of as holiness is nothing more than intolerance. This naïve approach to following God makes the Christian life seemingly simple: just exclude anyone who violates our image of the Christian life. Worship groups typically set up a code of behavior, rules for following God that take the guesswork out of discipleship. That view of the Christian life allows us to ascertain how we're doing by simply taking an inventory of our outward behavior.

Often what Christians think of as holiness is nothing more than intolerance. This naïve approach to following God makes the Christian life seemingly simple: just exclude anyone who violates our image of the Christian life.

One brief set of rules states, "Don't dance, drink, smoke or chew, or go with those girls who do." In theological terms these are called sins of *commission*. The problem with this view of holiness is that we can become oblivious to the primary sin Jesus was addressing in the above parable, sins of *omission*. We do not serve a performance-oriented deity but a God of mercy and forgiveness. Failing to carry out an act of mercy which we know God has placed before us amounts to disobedience and sin.

We can only guess at what the former lives of the priest and Levite were like. Perhaps they had dramatic conversion stories to tell; perhaps they had been raised in their respective traditions from birth. Regardless of their backgrounds, at this point in time they were both clearly out of touch with the world around them. Jesus used the priest and Levite as examples because, to some degree, we all practice the same sort of thinking that prompted them to walk past the wounded man.

While doing a seminar on kindness evangelism in the Kansas City area, we brainstormed about possible ways we could extend God's love into the community. We decided to be a bit different and go after a group that Christians would be unlikely to inter- sect—New Agers! A gathering of various New Age groups were sponsoring a "psychic fair" at the local convention center. Several hundred of the curious and devoted gathered for the weekend to grow in their knowledge of psychic phenomena.

We stationed ourselves in front of the convention center and gave away free soft drinks. Some members of the evangelism team were a bit fearful of the New Agers. For the most part, they had never spoken to anyone like that, but had read enough to be leary. To cope with our own fear and to disarm the conference attendees, we jokingly said, "We're giving away free soft drinks. Don't tell me ... I'm getting it clearly now. You want a diet Coke, right!?" The people coming into the auditorium were amused and many were open to talking with us further. I count that out- reach as especially significant because for the first time I stepped outside of my fears and over a line by speaking with people who believed very differently than I do.

Donald McGavern, professor at Fuller Seminary, coined the term "redemption and lift," one which aptly captures the Levite's mentality. While working in India, McGavern noticed a natural improvement in the quality of life of Hindus who came to know Christ. Once these new believers embraced a more biblical lifestyle, their lives became more stable socially, financially, and relationally. As followers of Jesus they spent their money differ- ently and tended to live more wisely in general. In short, they began to look more like Christ.

McGavern saw in this trend both a positive side and a negative side. As people were redeemed spiritually and uplifted in their quality of life, they tended to turn away from former relationships with outsiders and live strictly within a new circle of like-minded believers. The redeemed began to feel increasingly uncomfort- able relating to their non-Christian friends who held a very dif- ferent value system. In time they could easily fall prey to a subtle bias which often remains unverbalized: *These poor people around me wouldn't have as much pain in their lives if they were only as wise and together as I.*

Unless we are aware of this phenomenon of redemption and lift, we too will continue to stumble over the next wounded man the Lord lays at our feet. The farther we travel from our personal "B.C." days (Before Christ), the less we remain in touch with the reality of what life apart from Christ is really like. A spiritual arrogance or "sanctified amnesia" can soon settle upon the saints.

The longer we fellowship with other Christians apart from the reality of the world, the more we tend to exaggerate the darkness outside our church walls. We enjoy the Lord so much that we can't remember what it's like to be apart from God. We forget the balanced perspective of the psalmist, "If it had not been the Lord who was on our side ..." (Ps 124:1-3). In other words, "There but for the grace of God go I."

WHAT MYTHS KEEP YOU FROM REACHING OUT?

Was the Samaritan always so sensitive to the pain of others? Probably not. It would be unfair to assume that all Samaritans are sensitive or that all Levites and priests are necessarily dull of heart. The difference between these three men was that one had been freed from some stifling myths while the others were still bound by them. After two thousand years of church history, many of these same myths likely inhibit you and me from effectively reaching out as well.

What is a myth? Mark Twain said, "In life there are lies and then there are damn lies." In other words, there are blatant lies and subtle lies. A myth is a *subtle lie,* a belief close enough to the truth to be easily confused with pure truth. Myths are doubly dangerous to believers because we easily digest them as truth when we see them modeled by other Christians. When carried out and allowed to influence us over time, they can have a very poisoning effect on our hearts. Here are some religious myths many of us must struggle to overcome.

Myth number one: *My main function in evangelism is to invite nonbelievers to church.* Many Christians assume that if we have attractive facilities or well-oiled programs, then people will magically arrive at our doorstep. People who believe that myth haven't tried to start a church recently. For the most part, the unchurched of our communities really aren't looking for a church to join. In coming to Cincinnati I was told repeatedly, "There are already too many churches in this city." Although their conclusion may be debatable, the *perception* of the average unchurched person is that we already have plenty of churches in America.

Myth number two: *If a needy person asks me for help, I can excuse myself by apologizing, "Sorry, I don't have the gift of helping."* I suspect the Levite thought to himself, "That is not my ministry. I don't rank very high in mercy-giving. I'm more of a teacher. I'd be happy to do a study on the theme of mercy in the minor prophetic books, but I'm not really into the application stuff." Of course, some Christians will be called to more significant ministries of evangelism; a few will even function authentically in the office of evangelist. Paul, however, said that *every* believer is an ambassador for Christ (2 Cor 5:18-20). Jesus sent *us* into the world that the world may believe that God sent him (Jn 17:18-21).

Unfortunately, our attitude toward ministry has been influenced by the specialist mentality that marks our approach to medical services. Dawson Trotman, in his little booklet "Born to Reproduce," makes the excellent point that it is only natural for a healthy human being who is married to another healthy human being to reproduce children. Spiritually reproducing by bringing people into the family of God shouldn't be seen as something unusual at all, but rather as the norm for those who follow Christ.

When we see a needy person, we too often think (like the priest), *Someone really ought to do something about that person in* need over there. Of course, that is not my area of responsibility or gifting. I've taken a spiritual gifts test and I scored rather poorly in works of mercy. I'm all for people operating according to their greatest gifting, but my own track record tells me that I will regularly be called on to be Jesus to others smack-dab in the middle of my areas of weakness. In fact, God seems to provide training exercises just to help me learn and grow.

"Someone really ought to do something about that person in need over there. Of course, that is not my area of responsibility or gifting. I've taken a spiritual gifts test and I scored rather poorly in works of mercy."

For example, our church is attended by many smokers who congregate around the exit doors and then toss their cigarette butts on the ground. As a nonsmoker I don't understand that kind of behavior, but I do notice the butts lying around. For the past several years I have become by default the chief cigarette-butt-picker-upper. At first I wondered how "those insensitive smokers" could possibly not notice what they were doing. Now I believe that those butts are part of God's work of attitude-adjustment in my own life.

Myth number three: *This person doesn't look like a good candidate for conversion.* Upon hearing the basic idea of servant evangelism, one pastor responded with alarm: "What you're saying could be dangerous. I could see this thing getting out of hand. Before you know it the world would just be coming into the church. It seems things would get out of control pretty quickly."

I responded, "I don't mean to be disrespectful, but what you're describing is exactly the goal. My intention is to see that things do get out of hand. There is something refreshing about having more going on than one person can control."

The word "careful" implies that matters are in *our* hands instead of the Lord's. When the responsibility for a situation is resting upon our strength or capabilities, we will inevitably become "full of care" for the outcome. It is not my call or anyone else's to author or maintain the life of God in others. We can function as God's representatives but we cannot bear the responsibility for his people. God alone can "bring to completion" the good work that he has started (Phil 1:6). And I believe that what God has begun, he will maintain.

EVANGELISM SAMARITAN-STYLE

Jesus makes the Samaritan the hero of this parable—something which must have shocked the Jews listening to him. As the brunt of jokes in that day, Samaritans were stereotyped as simple, rural people who were slow and uneducated. Yet Jesus applauded this man's attitudes and actions as reflecting an accurate view of God's kingdom as a *merciful kingdom*. We learn from the Samaritan's example that when we step out to touch the lost, God's presence meets us and equips us to bring healing. In other words, the kingdom of God flows through those who are open to being dispensers of God's love and presence.

Jesus captures this thought when he quotes from Isaiah 61: "The Spirit of the Lord is upon me, because he has anointed me to preach ... to heal ... to set at liberty ... to proclaim ..." (Lk 4:18-19). We see that the inflow of the Lord's anointing is intricately tied to the outflow of our efforts to help others experience more of God's mercy. In fact, I have found that his presence and life are never more present than when I am giving away God's love to those who are hurting and lost. As we bring the message of God's mercy to the lost and needy, his anointing will be upon us as well to meet their needs.

The parable of the lost sheep (Lk 15:3-7) makes it clear that God highly values those who are not yet gathered into his fold. Scripture tells us that he rejoices more over the one who is lost and then found than over the ninety-nine already safe and sound.

Jesus modeled to us the outflowing of his kingdom wherever he went. He came to seek and to heal the lost—which included the sick lost, the imprisoned lost, the lame lost, or the poor lost. The Good Shepherd actively sought out unbelievers. In fact, he spent the better part of his ministry with those outside of established religion. And whenever Jesus was with the lost, he sensed the Father's very personal love for them and his desire to draw them into his kingdom.

In the same way, the Samaritan was anointed with God's grace when he stopped to help this wounded man. As he stepped out to show mercy to a stranger, he was loving the people that God is especially committed to. The priest and Levite experienced no such anointing because they didn't step out to give aid. My guess is that they hesitated to help because they didn't feel equipped or inspired. Maybe they were just tired. Had the priest and Levite taken the time to extend a helping hand, they would have found ample amounts of God's favor to meet their needs.

GETTING BEYOND OURSELVES

No matter how long we may have been stuck in wrong attitudes or approaches to the unchurched, we can still change. What practices can we build into our lives that would help us to share God's love more effectively? The following principles can be learned by reflecting on the actions of the priest, Levite, and Samaritan.

Be "with the people." If you long for more of God's heart, you'll probably get it simply by spending time with the unchurched. This phrase "with the people" is repeated often in the Book of Acts. Leaders of the early church were continually with the people, both inside and outside the fold of God. They lived out the opposite lifestyle from the priest and Levite, who believed that the secret to success meant being separated from the people. They believed that one could hear God more accurately by getting away from people.

The old preacher's adage seems true: "Either we will obey Acts 1:8, or we will experience Acts 8:1." In the first text, Jesus calls us to be his witnesses beginning in Jerusalem and on to Judea, Samaria, and ultimately to the ends of the earth. Acts 8:1 tells us that "on that day a great persecution arose against the church in Jerusalem; and they were all scattered throughout the region of Judea and Samaria."

Jesus sent his followers to sow the seeds of God's love to the ends of the earth, to dispel the grip of darkness by proclaiming the gospel. After some years it became obvious that most people were satisfied with sowing seeds in the same locale. No one wanted to leave Jerusalem and go to the ends of the earth. Consequently the local church had seeds piled up waist deep and going to waste. As South American evangelist Luis Palau says, Christians are a lot like fertilizer. Piled up in one place they will burn a hole in the ground beneath them. But spread out over a large field, they can do a lot of good!

One way or another, the Lord is intent on getting the church out of its own little circle and out into the presence of the world he loves. God is serious about wanting to reach the unleavened parts of our world with the good news of Jesus Christ.

Christians are a lot like fertilizer.
Piled up in one place they will burn a hole
in the ground beneath them. But spread out
over a large field, they can do a lot of good!

Step out of your comfort zone. In order to have any impact on the life of the wounded stranger, the Samaritan had to step out in faith. The Samaritan didn't seek to separate himself as the priest or Levite had. Rather, like Christ, he entered into the heart of the world and got involved in its pain face-to-face.

The Samaritan's actions reflect Jesus' image of the kingdom of God as comparable to a mustard seed: "It is like a mustard seed which, when it is sown on the ground, is smaller than all the seeds on earth; but when it is sown, it grows up, becomes greater than all herbs, and shoots out large branches, so that the birds of the air may nest under its shade" (Mk 4:31-32).

Christians tend to congregate. We are naturally drawn to community where we sense the strong presence of God. Community is part of what we are to be about, but a community of light without outward focus can quickly turn into a burned-out community. The purpose of light is defeated unless it penetrates the darkness. The nature of God within every believer is in direct conflict with any tendency we may have to hold onto the presence of God like a miser clutching gold.

Bring the kingdom. The Samaritan *brought* the kingdom of God as the answer to the wounded man's needs. He saw the kingdom of God as vital and living, reaching the pain of the lost and touching them directly. Jesus didn't *send* the truth and life of God; he *became* the truth and life. He entered the plane of humanity to show us what human life could be like when it was centered on God's love. Jesus didn't send the love of God; he brought that love to those who were in need.

My hunch is that the Samaritan suffered some immediate accusations because of his involvement with the wounded man. We too will sometimes be misunderstood as we step out to share God's love. For some time now I have been going to a local abortion clinic and demonstrating God's love to those on both sides of the abortion issue. I am definitely against abortion, but I feel that the best way to soften hard hearts is to enter the situation with the power of kindness. I have given out free coffee and soft drinks and washed the windshields of everyone there.

The pro-abortion people think I'm a little weird. They may be thinking, "We know he's up to something, we just haven't figured it out yet." The Christians on the other hand have often been less than graceful toward me. I often hear catcalls, "Next time bring your anti-abortion sign with you." Anti-abortion activists see no point in what we are doing and suspect our stance on abortion as being soft.

Mother Teresa has dealt with misunderstanding like this for years. She captures a wonderful balance when she describes the mission of the Sisters of Charity: "We are contemplatives that live in the heart of the world twenty-four hours a day." The Samaritan exhibited this same balance and Jesus identified him as a hero.

Begin to care. It sounds simple, but we can decide to open our hearts and begin to care. We can decide to allow our hearts to become sensitive again to the pain of others. God has shaped our hearts to notice the needs that grieve him. Wherever our hearts have become hardened over the years, they can become softened and pliable again. Begin with a simple prayer. Ask God to give you his heart, to help you see the way he sees.

It is one thing to see and quite another to notice. The priest and Levite *saw* the beaten man with their eyes, but they really didn't *notice*. The Samaritan's heart was sensitive to noticing the pain of others. We would be mistaken to think that the good Samaritan was going through life just looking for someone to help. He was apparently a businessman, someone used to schedules and appointments. He was probably on a business trip, traveling an established trade route, one known to the bandits as well. He may have passed that way on many other occasions, as evidenced by the reaction of the innkeeper. I'm sure that he had important affairs on his mind, but he put them aside because he cared about this stranger in need.

Make yourself available. Begin in prayer, then look for those God will send your way. The Lord is looking for people who want to be used by him to carry his mercy to the world. He hears the cry of our hearts whenever we pray, but God seems especially receptive to prayers of availability. I have challenged many people over the years to begin their trek toward greater usefulness by asking God to send them opportunities. I have seldom met someone who didn't see immediate and encouraging answers to that sort of prayer.

While doing a seminar in Baton Rouge, a pastor confided in me that he had been stuck inside the four walls of the church for some years. Excited about this idea of kindness evangelism, he wondered if he could break out of his personal safety zone. After participating in a large soft drink outreach at an LSU football game, this man came back very enthused at what he'd seen. His group of twenty-five had given away over six hundred drinks to those driving into the stadium parking lot.

During lunch this pastor confessed to me that he had spent most of his Christian life maintaining the same fears he had as a non-Christian. In particular he had harbored a fear of the black community. He couldn't offer a rational explanation, but for years he had held a disdain for the blacks of his city. That day, as he gave away soft drinks, something broke in him. The last I talked to this pastor, he told me he had built a shoeshine kit and regularly visited a local grocery market on Saturday mornings to offer free shoeshines. Many of his customers were black men. As he made himself available, the fears that had kept him captive for years dissipated.

Many of us started out our Christian walk
with an availability that said, "Whatever, Lord."
Then somewhere along the way,
we lost this gambler's attitude.

Many of us started out our Christian walk with an attitude of availability, an approach to life that said, "Whatever, Lord." Convinced that God's power could change any human heart, we were willing to risk all to be obedient to Christ. Then somewhere along the way, we lost this gambler's attitude. Disappointments, unrealistic expectations, and the trauma of life slowly took the wind from our sails. Perhaps our enthusiasm was dented by watching other believers with what we considered to be a far less available and obedient attitude.

Now is the time to return to our first love for Christ. For me the key has been to realize that if I wait until all of my questions are answered and all of my problems are healed, then I will never get launched into ministry to the lost. I must be willing to live with some tension between my current lack and God's promise of provision.

Manage your fear by going with a group. I go out to do kindness evangelism at least once per week. Having maintained this schedule for many years now, I am still a bit fearful every time I go out. My hunch is that we will never be completely free from our fears. They are simply part of the human predicament. In order to overcome them, we must find fellowship in our fears. When we go out to do ministry, I tell my people, "We can be afraid together and go out into the community."

Most of the people I speak to about doing kindness evangelism don't realize that I'm fearful most of the time when going out to do ministry. I score as an introvert on personality inventories. I also have a low need for adventure. The ideal workday for me is being in an office alone working uninterruptedly on projects. Recognizing that I will always have to deal with my fear to some extent, I will be wiser to seek to *manage* my fears of interacting with unbelievers. I became more effective as a leader when I stopped looking for fear*less* people and just began to work with others who are willing to manage their fears along with me. The key is being in a group where we can more readily sense God's presence. Also, courage is contagious.

I was in Queens, New York, teaching for several days at New Life Fellowship. After talking about evangelism each morning, we went out into the community for several hours of hands-on practice. We experimented with several servant evangelism projects to get an idea of what would work in this section of the Big Apple. One rather large team enthusiastically took on a free car wash. Remarkably, in four hours they washed two hundred fifty cars.

A skeptical taxi driver slowed down and yelled out, "Why in the *@*! are you fooling people? That's not very &%#! nice for you Christians to lie to people by telling them you're washing cars free when you're really not."

One man holding a sign announcing the car wash responded back, "It really is free. We really mean it. No donations accepted. We're doing this just to show you that God loves you incredibly." The man was incredulous and drove on.

Two minutes later he came back, rolled his window down, and asked, "Is this *really* free?" After one more assurance, he pulled in and let us begin to wash his car even though he was still a little skeptical. A few moments later the pace of cars pulling in picked up and even those carrying the signs went to work washing. The skeptical taxi driver volunteered to hold one of the "Free Car wash—No Kidding" signs. In true New York taxi driver fashion he was yelling as people drove by, "Hey you, get in here! It really is free! I didn't believe them either, but they really are doing this just to show you God's love!" Out of the mouths of babes ... or hardened taxi drivers.

Realize that failure is a given. I believe the priest in Jesus' story was profoundly fearful of failure. "I might step out to do something and fall flat on my face." That is a realistic fear. My encouragement to you is that you *will* fall flat on your face. Failure is predictable! Realizing that fact gives me a lot of courage.

A message I frequently repeat to our leaders and workers is this: "Isn't it wonderful that we can obey the call to do evangelism realizing that failure is just around the corner? The only unknown in our outreach is *how* we're going to fail and exactly *when* we're going to fail." We have taken as our motto a saying of George Bernard Shaw: "Anything worth doing is worth doing wrong." Ours is not to demand success but to see every opportunity as a learning experience that will mold us into more capable servants for Christ.

I sometimes feel like Dorothy and her friends in *The Wizard of Oz*. As they continued on their journey, they began to focus on everything that might go wrong and began to chant, "Lions, tigers, and bears, oh my!" Not one vicious lion, tiger, or bear ever appeared during the whole trip. As in that movie, most of our fears never materialize.

This timeless story taps into our experiences of entering into the world: it is a scary and overwhelming place, especially at first. As with Dorothy, few of our fears are as bad as we first think. When she finally encountered the enemy face to face, Dorothy discovered that the wicked witch was not so powerful after all. Just a little water finished her off.

In my years of going out into the community, I have discovered that the *fear* of failure is much worse than failure itself. A recent survey asked several hundred American men to name their number one fear. I was surprised to learn the results. I thought that fear of death would be at the top, but it came in fourth. The fear of growing bald was even further down the list. The number one anxiety of American men was the fear of losing their jobs. A follow-up survey six months later queried the men who had actually lost their jobs. Consistently the respondents indicated that *losing their jobs* was one of the most positive things that had ever happened to them. Many discovered new careers they had long dreamed about but been fearful of venturing into as long as they were employed. When we turn and face our fears, we discover that the dread of loss is truly stronger than the loss itself.

Sow liberally. In ancient times sowing seed was done very differently than it is today. Modern farmers first plow to break up the hard soil and then sow the seed. In Jesus' day seed was thrown and *then* the soil was plowed. Wherever seed was flung, there would be action of some sort later on.

When we plant a seed of love, we can be assured that some of God's presence will be deposited. At some point in time, depending on many variables, that seed will hopefully grow to produce a plant. The fact that some soil was rocky, full of weeds, or shallow did not preclude its receiving seed and producing some growth. The best soil and the right conditions of light, soil, and weeding produced the most growth, but the farmer in Jesus' parable did not limit his sowing to good soil alone.

When I was ten, my brother and I planted a backyard garden at our home in Wichita, Kansas. Our mom let us plant our sections of the garden however we wanted. I carefully read the directions on the back of the seed packet and even looked in an encyclopedia to find out how carrots should be planted. My rows were straight, orderly, parallel—just like the instructions said they should be. In fact, I did everything right ... except for one detail: I planted my seeds too deep in the soil.

Erik was four at the time and had a very different approach to planting than I did. He took the entire contents of his two seed packets and threw them on the ground over a one square foot diameter. After several weeks we had two very different gardens. Erik had dozens of pencil-sized carrots in his, while I had nothing to show for my careful, hard work. I discovered later that I had planted my carrots about an inch too deep. My brother had hardly planted his seeds, but because they were fertile they basically rooted themselves in the good soil. Erik's approach wasn't pretty, but it did produce an abundance of carrots.

We need to be a little more like Erik in our approach to evangelism. The most important lesson that we can draw from the story of the sower is that God's presence follows the seeds that are planted and bestows power and blessing on the seed apart from the sower. The key is understanding that life is in the seed itself. The sower's role was to fling the seed—hopefully on good ground. With an abundance of seed available, he was unconcerned about the results.

Jesus called all who would hear him to come into the family of God. He came "to seek and to save that which was lost" (Lk 19:10). To "seek" means to "invite in." We can assume that God is actively drawing everyone to himself, whether they look like they're responding or not. There are no categories of people, some that he's calling and some he's not. God's desire is to include the entire human race in his family, even the most unlikeable villains on the planet. "The Lord is ... not willing that any should perish but that all should come to repentance" (2 Pt 3:9). Not everyone will respond to his invitation, but God's attitude remains the same.

Our job is to be seed flingers,
not seed protectors watching over God's business
as though he had a limited supply.

◆◆◆

In a recent Clint Eastwood western, the main character has a couple of gun-slinging allies. They are all major tough guys, of course, but one of them has a humorous twist: he is incredibly nearsighted and can't shoot straight. The remedy? Shoot in all directions, reload, and continue shooting. He figures that he is bound to hit something eventually if he just keeps at it. The attitude of this shooter is similar to the approach of the sower in the parable. God has no shortage of bullets or seed. We have tended to underestimate his resources and proceeded more like Barney Fife on the *Andy Griffith Show*—as though we had just one bullet! We can let loose and shoot in all directions because we have an infinite supply of ammunition.

Our job is to be seed flingers, not seed protectors watching over God's business as though he had a limited supply. If we are sowing the seed of God's kingdom, there will be no shortage of seed. As soon as we sow what we have, there is more in its place. The value for sowing liberally is captured in Ecclesiastes 11:1-2: "Cast your bread upon the waters, for you will find it after many days. Give a serving to seven, and also to eight, for you do not know what evil will be on the earth." We cast the bread and God causes the results.

When I began to do evangelism, I saw myself as a sower to whom God had granted a small amount of seed to sow. Assuming I had only a thimbleful of seed to last me a lifetime, I would be foolish to plant any except in the most fertile places. Consequently, I sowed God's love carefully and sparingly—much as I had my small garden plot in Kansas. I came to realize deeds of love are meant to be sown in a broadcast fashion, as modeled by the sower in Jesus' parable.

SOWING EVERYWHERE, EVEN PINKIE'S BAR

Every Saturday morning at ten is a special time at our church, the time when groups go out into the community to serve in practical ways. Some take food and clothing to the poor, others do various servant evangelism projects. One Saturday I was with a team that was washing the windows of businesses in downtown Cincinnati, including retail stores, restaurants, and even an occasional bar.

On this particular Saturday, my last stop was Pinkie's Bar. It was about noon and the place was full of customers, with Waylon Jennings "wayling" on the corner jukebox. This was no classy place—beer was served in the can. I asked the woman tending bar if I could wash their front windows as a simple expression of God's love. With little reaction she said, "Whatever turns you on."

As I began to clean the windows with a teammate, a group of four customers called me over to the bar. "We heard what you said to the bartender about doing this to show God's love. We want to know what kind of church would do something like this."

I spent several minutes telling them about our fellowship. Then a woman with tears brimming in her eyes asked, "Do you think people like us would fit into a church like yours?"

Recalling this story serves as a wonderful progress check for me. Several years ago I probably would have instantly answered, "Yes, of course!" But the disdain in my voice would have caused her to question whether she was really invited. My heart would have said, "We're Christians. Don't you know that's what Christians do? We love people!" If she had come, however, she would have met people who wouldn't have necessarily welcomed her into their hearts. She would have encountered people influenced by the myths and fears we've discussed in this chapter. My own false perceptions about non-Christians had convinced me at one point that only the lowest forms of life on the planet hang around bars.

God has since shown me a different kind of love, a fertile love that reaches out toward everyone. For years I loved the lost in obedience to God and his Word. In recent years something has shifted in my heart. I feel I've grown. Now I don't just love the lost, I even like them.

FIVE DISCOVERIES THAT EMPOWER EVANGELISM

*"When strangers start acting like neighbors ...
communities are reinvigorated."*
—Ralph Nader

*"If there is any kindness I can show, or any good
thing I can do to any fellow being, let me do it now,
and not deter or neglect it,
as I shall not pass this way again."*
—William Penn

I TOOK MY FIRST STAB at premeditated kindness by organizing a free car wash while my wife Janie and I were starting a church in Oslo, Norway. The first customer's bumper sticker identified the driver as a member of the Socialist

Agnostic political party. Our Norwegian friends felt utterly incapable of talking to this woman for fear she would come at them with mind-boggling arguments they'd be unable to answer.

The worst fear of all Scandinavians was being realized: the possibility of looking bad in public. It had taken me six weeks to convince this small group that an outreach would be "big fun" and now they were not having one bit of fun. Even though I spoke Norwegian with a noticeable accent, I engaged our customer in conversation. "Hi, we're going to wash your car for free and we're not going to allow you to give us any money for this."

"OK, but why?"

"We want to show you God's love in a tangible way. His love is free and so is ours!" I said.

By the time we finished washing her car, to the amazement of the Norwegian Christians, this lady was weeping. She was experiencing reverse sticker shock—we *wouldn't* take her money. She rolled down the window and said, "I am fifty years old and have lived in a so-called Christian nation all my life. I've heard people talk and talk and talk about God for a long time and have opposed them. I determined a long time ago they weren't real in their love, so he must not be real. But today, this is the first time I have *experienced* any of God's love. What I have seen here is real!"

> *"I am fifty years old and have lived in a so-called Christian nation all my life. I've heard people talk and talk and talk about God for a long time and have opposed them. But today, this is the first time I have experienced any of God's love."*

As she pulled away two Mormon missionaries drove up. Their clip-on black ties, little black name tags, white shirts, and distinctive short haircuts gave them away from a distance. As we washed their car these young missionaries from Utah were also surprised we wouldn't take their money.

"So why are you doing this?" they asked.

"Just to show you God's love in a practical way." I had never met a speechless Mormon missionary. All those I had met over the years are not one bit shy about giving their memorized speech, but we had two dumbfounded Mormon missionaries standing before us. They had nothing to say because we had beaten them to the punch with a demonstration of the reality of God that no verbal comeback could match.

Janie and I learned many valuable lessons from that year in Norway. We learned about enduring in the midst of difficulty, keeping on with a project even without much response, and doing what we do as unto the Lord and not to people. St. John of the Cross, in his book *Dark Night of the Soul,* explains how God allows all of us to go through trauma and testing in order to bring us to new levels of dependence upon him.[1] God even allows us to feel abandoned by him and others so that we will grow in faithfulness regardless of our emotions. This author suggests that all of us go through those "dark nights" occasionally because we don't grow spiritually except in times of adversity.

Our dark night of the soul occurred during our year in Norway. True to the prediction of St. John of the Cross, we emerged from this time of isolation with important spiritual and emotional growth under our belts. We had to develop a "never-say-die" attitude in Norway because the people there were not looking for what we had to offer. We came to Cincinnati in 1983 thinking it would be different. We were wrong.

THE HOWARD BEALE EXPERIENCE

Cincinnati is friendly, but in a skeptical kind of way. New ideas don't catch on quickly here. I noticed when we first moved here that Cincinnatians wear belts and suspenders at the same time, clear evidence of conservatism. Mark Twain wrote over one hundred years ago, "When the end of time comes, I want to be in Cincinnati because everything happens ten years later there."

Not only was the weather cold, damp, and unwelcoming to two former Californians, but we also found the people skeptical of the new ideas we presented. Our new fellowship grew at a snail's pace. From my early Christian days as part of the Jesus Movement, I was conditioned to think my job was to open the Bible and automatically large crowds would assemble. I was wrong.

I felt a lot like Howard Beale, a main character in the movie entitled *Network*. This veteran newsman is unexpectedly given the option to retire or be fired to make room for a more youthful replacement. Instead of offering the expected niceties in his last editorial comment on the air, Beale begins to talk from his heart. He voices frustration over his sense of ineffectiveness in life and confesses that he has been ruled by his fears.

As his career comes to a close, Howard Beale expresses remorse that he spent his life playing roles and knuckling under to everyone's expectations around him. Now, on his last day at work, he decides to express the depths of his heart. His swan song concludes with the exhortation, "Wherever you are, I want you to get up, go to your window, open it, and yell as loudly as you can, 'I'm mad as hell and I'm *not* going to take it anymore!'" Seemingly all of New York City promptly joins in with this one man's chorus of rebellion.

Howard Beale was stuck on a skip in the record that seemed to play over and over, "Play out your expected role." He never explored or discovered who he really was. That approach to life can only be lived out so long, until one comes to a crisis or something inside of us dies. Beale finally decided to reveal his heart and convictions without caring whether the critics around him approved or not.

I found myself at that same point in my own life. I was tired of being careful about starting this new church and making sure it was done the "right" way. I was frustrated at my own sense of ineffectiveness, at my unwillingness to take the risky route to evangelism that Jesus seemed to always take. For most of my Christian life the message had played loud and clear, "Play the expected role."

I had been stuck in a mode of perpetual preparation—continually getting ready for the work of God's kingdom, acquiring equipment for spiritual warfare that would never be used unless I got outside the castle walls. As a leader I was very focused on the idea of getting the people properly prepared. My life's motto could have been phrased, "Ready, aim ... Ready, aim ... Ready, aim...." I was stuck in a state of perpetual readiness. I never got to "fire."

"Fire" meant stepping out to change. Like many Christians, I was fearful of obeying the Lord—afraid of change, afraid of failure, afraid of disappointment if things didn't go well. I would have never admitted to resisting the forward progress of God's kingdom, but my fearful attitude toward change served as a continual blockage. My vision was so small and narrow it made me and what I was doing seem boring and unattractive to outsiders. As low as our numbers were, I was still fearful of losing the little that we had accumulated.

My life's motto could have been phrased,
"Ready, aim ... Ready, aim ... Ready, aim...."
I was stuck in a state of perpetual readiness.
I never got to "fire."

The changing point for me came while sitting at a restaurant one day. I had just shared my vision for starting this new church—and had been rejected once again—when I felt the Lord speak to me. He said volumes in just a short space: *"If you will befriend my friends, I will send you more people than you will know what to do with."*

I had no idea who God's "friends" were, but those words

proved to be a turning point in my heart and in our fledgling church. Sheer desperation pushed me to see the Christian life and evangelism in new ways. Over the next several weeks I searched the Scriptures, prayed, and asked, "Who are God's friends?" I began to see a trend in the New Testament texts that I hadn't noticed before. Though Jesus loved everybody, he apparently *enjoyed* some people more than others. His heart especially went out to the poor, the sick, and the lost. Even the twelve men Jesus chose as his disciples (with the exception of Judas Iscariot) were from Galilee, the poor section of Palestine.

I knew that my job was to minister to the hurting but didn't know how. I had done plenty of door-knocking and knew it didn't work for me. Besides, people were more skeptical of the Church than ever. After all, hadn't I already received several hundred rejections to my invitation of being involved in this new fellowship?

Then a new idea began to form. If I could somehow relieve an ounce of the pain someone was going through, maybe then we could get that person's attention. If our church could meet people on the basis of serving our way into their hearts, maybe then we would have an audience. Servant evangelism was born out of this realization that as we touch people at their point of pain— whether the need was for food, healing, or wisdom—they would open the door of their hearts and invite us into their lives.

I had come to Cincinnati with the wrong goal. My ambition of starting a new church was much too narrow. The goal that was worth pursuing was much more central to the heart of God: to bring the kingdom of God to this city through acts of love and mercy. Everything in the Christian life flows out of the first commandment: to love God with our heart, soul, strength, and mind. That *vertical love,* from God to us, lays the foundation for any other love. *Horizontal love* for our neighbor overflows out of the love of God.

Once I believed in a goal that was worth accomplishing, I was beginning to have God's heart. Consequently, my internal orders started to change. The new assignment was to find ways to relieve people's pain. But how could I encounter these people? How could I overcome their skepticism, their tendency to misinterpret any attempts to reach out to them? Let me share with you five discoveries that empowered me to bring Christ to others.

1. PEOPLE LISTEN WHEN I TREAT THEM LIKE FRIENDS

Even though we saw the power of kindness in our first attempt at servant evangelism in Oslo, the results were scarce. That same project in Cincinnati bore fruit immediately. We displayed several banners reading "ABSOLUTELY FREE CAR WASH—NO MONEY ACCEPTED." A couple of former cheerleaders stood on the corner with signs directing dirty cars to our crew. The rest of the team waited to begin washing, cleaning windows and tires, and vacuuming. We also had a couple of designated talkers to share *why* we were doing this. Lots of people drove by with a jaded look on their face as if to say, "Right. I'm sure this is free. Nothing is really for free. There's got to be a catch."

Our first customer was a haggard-looking, single mom with a half dozen squirming kids in an old station wagon. We could see in her eyes that life had been hard on her. We gave her a cold drink and explained our project while her car was washed from top to bottom. Before leaving she asked for prayer and cried a little as we asked God to begin to show himself to her. This mother left with a smile on her face. It was clear that our small gift of service had turned her day around.

The second car that pulled in was a stainless steel Delorean sports car whose gray-haired driver was a well-known, wealthy Cincinnatian. "How much?" he asked.

"It's free," we answered. The man nodded slightly with a quizzical look.

As we finished, he asked, "To whom shall I make out my check?"

"No, sir," someone told him again, "we really aren't taking

any money for washing your car. We did this just because God loves you." He repeated himself and began to show some signs of irritation that we were so slow in understanding his simple question. For the third time, I told him we wouldn't take his money because this really was a *free* car wash. To my surprise tears welled up in his eyes. In a world full of the "work-hard-and-then-you-are-rewarded" approach to life, our free gift seemed beyond reason. This man seemed very touched.

Many other people were strongly touched that afternoon in a way mere talk couldn't accomplish. We closed our time in prayer and shed a few tears of gratefulness for God's favor. After three hours we had washed over forty cars. Someone commented to me, "Jesus was right. It really is more blessed to give than receive." That day we began to see and feel the pain of those we served. We sensed our hearts being enlarged and looking more like his than when we'd begun. Most important, we had made a lasting discovery: people respond to the message of the church when we approach them as friends.

Excluders or includers. German sociologist Ferdinand Tonnies authored a famous book in the 1800s called *Gemeinschaft und Gesellschaft*. In this study the author identified small communities as being built on one-to-one relationships and the exclusive sense of a small family as *gemeinschaft*. On the other hand, the *gesellschaft* approach to relationships operates on the basis of inclusion.

The first sort of relationships are cozy but exclusive. *Gemeinschaft* groups typically appear to be friendly, but they quickly deny access to newcomers who are different. The thinking here is, *I cannot associate with you unless you become like me. You must leave your circle and join mine, for I am unwilling to change.* These primary groups are nearly impossible to invade unless newcomers are capable of adapting to their established social standards.

One of the most common ways Christians exclude outsiders is through our language. Newcomers catch on very quickly as to whether our fellowships are open or closed by what kind of jargon we use. The following extreme renditions of some simple sayings may give you some idea as to how outsiders may feel when they listen to us:

Dead men tell no tales: "Male cadavers are incapable of yielding any testimony."

Cleanliness is next to godliness: "Freedom from encrustations of grime is contiguous to rectitude."

Look before you leap: "Surveillance should precede saltation."

Twinkle, twinkle, little star: "Scintillate, scintillate, asteroid minifid."

He who laughs last, laughs best: "Abstention from presenting the ultimate cachination possesses thereby the optimal cachination."

While the *gemeinschaft* approach shrinks the opening to a group, the *gesellschaft* approach creates a funnel which makes it easy for an individual to gain entry. It's as if all of us have a funnel of some size resting over our heads, with the size of the opening determined by the size of our hearts. If we are seeking to be includers like Jesus, we will experience ever-growing funnels which are receptive to new people and new ideas. If we live as excluders, our shrinking funnels will keep out more than we allow into our lives.

Jesus says, "Whoever comes to me I will never drive away" (Jn 6:37). "Whoever" meant that all were welcome to be his friends. His funnel was large enough to encompass us all. Throughout his life, Jesus made a habit of hanging around with unpopular people like prostitutes, outlaws, the poor, the diseased, the demonized—not the crowd most of us spend time with every day. Yet they were open to Jesus and to his message. That's what counted.

Because they were open to being loved by him, God extended his love to them.

Since Jesus' love and acceptance includes everyone, we all need to be constantly striving to increase the capacity of our hearts. To the degree that we love and accept people the way they are, without preconditions or culturally prescribed expectations, to that degree we love the way God loves. Our hearts are never static; they are either growing or shrinking. The bench-mark of an expanding heart is one that is *unoffendable* by those who are different. To keep our hearts growing, we must walk in the *agape* or unconditional love Jesus showed us in the miracles he performed, and ultimately, demonstrated on the cross.

2. WHEN I SERVE, HEARTS ARE TOUCHED

One evening in the mid-sixties I was out in the car with my dad having a father and son talk—something we usually did the day report cards came out. I was no honor roll student then, but this was a particularly poor grading period for me. Trying to be constructive in his criticism, my dad referred to the attendant at the gas station as an example. "Steve, you've got to do better with your grades if you expect to get anywhere in life. If you don't start doing better," Dad said, pointing to the man washing the windshield, "you're going to end up washing windshields and cleaning toilets for a living when you grow up." As it turns out, he was a prophet and didn't know it!

My dad's image of people who serve in menial ways is pretty common, typified by Goober on the *Andy Griffith Show.* Goober manned the gas pumps at the local gas station, checked oil levels, and washed windshields. A man who took pleasure in the simple things in life, Goober was negatively portrayed as a simple-minded guy with little hope for a better future. Our culture often paints such a picture of people who serve—as slow, uneducated people who couldn't make anything of themselves and ended up taking whatever work they could find. We might speak disdain-fully of someone saying, "Cousin Bob works with his hands," meaning he couldn't get any other work.

◆◆◆

"Steve, if you don't start getting better grades,"
Dad said, pointing to the man washing the
windshield, "you're going to end up washing
windshields and cleaning toilets for a living
when you grow up." As it turns out, he was a
prophet and didn't know it!

◆◆◆

That attitude may represent the thinking of the world system, but it is the opposite of the scriptural model. As Christians, it is our nature to serve. We are indwelled by the Holy Spirit, that same Spirit who lived through Jesus while he walked the earth. Paul concisely describes Jesus' life and ministry in terms of a ser-vant: "Let this mind be in you which was also in Christ Jesus, who, being in the form of God, did not consider it robbery to be equal with God, but made himself of no reputation, taking the form of a servant, and coming in the likeness of men. And being found in appearance as a man, he humbled himself and became obedient to the point of death, even the death of the cross" (Phil 2:5-8).

When we come to Christ, God grants us a new nature which is entirely different from our old self-centered one that sought to be served. As we encounter the life of God, we come to have the same nature as that of Jesus Christ. As we live out that nature by serving others, we are able to influence the lives of others.

The call of God is in direct opposition to our cultural condi-tioning. I was raised in an upper-middle-class, ethnic home that valued hard work. The unspoken motto of my Scandinavian rela-tives was, "You get what you work for." I grew to see the poor, the sick, and the lost as people who were getting what they had worked for—and what they deserved. My oversimplified view of life told me that my family did well because we were wise and hardworking.

John 13 records the events of the Last Supper, a clear example of the priority Jesus placed on serving. Gayle Erwin explores the significance of this meeting in his book, *The Jesus Style:*

> Imagine Jesus, biceps bulging beneath a seamless robe with flowing cape, reclining at supper with his disciples. The forces of evil have been collecting for months and are about to kill him, but don't worry, all the power ever created is coursing through his body. He gets up—this man surrounded by overwhelming evil forces—walks over to the disciples and with all this incredible power ... begins to do what? "He got up from the meal, took off his outer clothing, and wrapped a towel around his waist. After that, he poured water into a basin and began to wash his disciples' feet...." So that is what he does with power! He washes feet.[2]

The arena of the heart. We can choose to do battle in two different arenas. We can either try to convince others in the arena of the *mind* or we can approach people in the arena of the *heart.* For the most part, traditional approaches to evangelism go head-to-head instead of heart-to-heart. We assume that if we could just get unbelievers to *think* straight, then we would see them come to Christ. Having equated salvation with a mental assent to particular doctrines, we try to enter peoples' lives by way of argumentation.

The mind certainly plays a part in coming to Christ, but the will is central in what Scripture frequently refers to as the heart. The *Evangelical Dictionary of Theology* defines "heart" in the biblical sense as meaning "the center or focus of man's personal life, the spring of all his desires, motives, and moral choices—indeed, of all his behavioral trends." Thus, when we touch the heart, we have touched a person at the deepest level.

The exciting news is that the heart isn't unreachable. Our experience has shown that a person's heart is most quickly touched by acts of service. A Norwegian expression wonderfully captures this idea: *"kjokken veien"* or "the kitchen way in." In other words, coming in the back door, the pleasant, easy door. This kitchen-door entrance with the gospel revolves around acts of practical service. In other words, we truly enter the lives of others in evangelism when we touch their hearts.

Though we may use other entry points—perhaps appealing to people's minds or emotions—ultimately we must, according to Scripture, invade their hearts. And the sooner we get to the heart of those we are seeking to lead to Jesus, the better able we are to connect with them at their core. Servant evangelism enables us to quickly touch the heart—the decision-making center of a person's life—and make a lasting impact. If the human heart is the ultimate target of our evangelism, why not shoot for the heart from the first moment of our encounter with non-Christians?

3. As I Serve, I Redefine the Perception of a Christian

A small group leader from a church in eastern Canada told me about his experience in front of a local donut shop. His group was washing windshields in the parking lot when they noticed several customers watching them. After some discussion inside the shop, a sharply dressed businessman came out. With a British accent he said, "We've been watching you from inside the shop washing our windshields and were just wondering why you're doing this."

The leader answered, "We're showing God's love to you by cleaning your windshields for free."

He gave a classic British response, "Jolly good!" The business-man then went back inside and told the others. Heads were shaking, people were waving, and then some further discussion followed. From the smiles on the customers' faces, this group knew they had succeeded in redefining what it meant to be a

Christian. In the eyes of those donut shop customers, Christians were those who debate and ask for donations.

Serving is a catalyst for the kingdom of God to go forward into the world. Our credibility grows as we walk in servanthood, and the greater our authority, the more the world will listen to our message. We have known more of promotion than we have of true authority. Recent church history tells us that very gifted people don't always wield great power and influence.

Jesus was empowered precisely because he came as a servant. Philippians 2:9-11 tells us the end result: "Therefore God also has highly exalted him and given him the name which is above every name, that at the name of Jesus every knee should bow, of those in heaven, and of those on earth, and of those under the earth, and that every tongue should confess that Jesus Christ is Lord, to the glory of God the Father." As the ultimate servant, Jesus received ultimate authority from the Father. Because he had authority in the lives of those he served, Jesus was able to call people to repentance.

Mother Teresa has been one of the most influential people on the earth because she has served perhaps more than anyone. Tony Campolo describes Mother Teresa's appearance at a Harvard University chapel service. She didn't pull any punches. At one point she said, "I understand there are lots of you students in this school who are doing things that displease God. You are harming yourselves and offending God. Some of you are drinking alcohol and taking drugs. Others of you are engaged in sexual sin of many sorts. I have a message for you from God: Repent, turn away from what you are doing."

The result of Mother Teresa's exhortation was amazing. The entire auditorium full of people rose to their feet and applauded thunderously for several minutes. They gave this simple woman a standing ovation for calling them to repentance! Her credibility as a servant gave her authority as a speaker.

Servanthood leads to authority and success in the business world as well. According to an article in *The New York Times*, Japanese donut makers have discovered the power of serving through their own experience.

It can be argued that anyone who opens a Mister Donut franchise in Japan really wants to. On the first day of management training, the future entrepreneurs are sent by bus to a Kyoto residential district, where they go from house to house, knocking on doors and politely asking permission to scrub the family toilet.... The spirit of thanksgiving is not dead in the Mister Donut operation today—and it also pinpoints the difference between Japan's Mister Donut and its American counterpart. Each year on January 27, the day it was decided to introduce Mister Donut in Japan, every shop manager, sales person, and baker in the Japanese operation is dispatched to clean a public washroom in the spirit of "self-reflection and gratitude," as a company leaflet describes it.[3]

When people express a desire to love as Jesus does, I usually ask them if they are willing to serve others in practical ways, even if they know that person will never come to know Christ. When they're willing to serve without regard for the response, then I know they're beginning to move in the love of God.

4. DOING THE MESSAGE PRECEDES TELLING THE MESSAGE

As I mentioned earlier in the book, our church has offered free gift wrapping as an outreach at area malls during the past several Christmas seasons. During our first year, we wrapped gifts for the two weeks before Christmas and managed to serve and talk to about ten thousand people. Claire, a recently divorced woman, was one of them. Impressed that we wouldn't take any money for our services, she took a card with our fellowship's name, location, and service times listed. She thanked us and left.

Shortly after that day at the mall, Claire visited our church. After the service she told me that she had thoroughly enjoyed herself, then left, and didn't return for nearly eighteen months. Then suddenly, Claire came back. Since then, she's been making friends and attending our meetings on a regular basis. Once, we asked her to describe to everyone how she had come to our fellowship. Claire stood in front of the congregation and spoke in a soft, quiet voice.

"I first learned about this church a couple of years ago when I had my Christmas gifts wrapped at the mall. Because of things that had gone on in my past, I was fearful of Christians and churches in general. If you had attempted to tell me anything about Jesus then, I would have run away as quickly as possible in the opposite direction. Instead, you wrapped my presents for me, you asked how my shopping was going, and you let me see that you cared about me. You did all that without asking for money or anything else. When I saw that, I realized that I didn't need to be afraid anymore."

By serving this woman and putting the ball "back into her court," we opened a door for the Lord to begin working in her heart. That work, Claire says, went on quietly for over a year—until she was "ripe" for harvesting. This divorced mother of two now has a personal relationship with Jesus and is growing from regular fellowship with other believers.

"If you had attempted to tell me anything about Jesus then, I would have run away as quickly as possible in the opposite direction. Instead, you wrapped my presents for me, you asked how my shopping was going, and you let me see that you cared about me."

For too long we have been insensitive to people's readiness to embrace Christ. We have tended to treat everyone as though they are equally open to the idea of becoming a Christian. That's not true. Had we run roughshod over Claire at the wrapping booth, she would have chalked up the experience as another negative encounter with overly excited Christians. Cornering her with information about how she could get right with God would have been what she was expecting, with a head-to-head attempt to overcome all of her reasons for resisting Christ.

At one time I thought the person with the best argument was declared the winner. After talking to lots of non-Christians over the years, I have come to see that most arguments about the gospel don't go very far in bringing people to Christ. When Christians come across as argumentative, we are often perceived as being unloving and harsh. Those few unbelievers who like to argue are typically going to believe what they want to believe—no matter how persuasive an evangelist happens to be.

I believe that the process of coming to Jesus Christ is more like the concept of falling in love with the person you'll eventually marry. In fact, this metaphor of the Church as the bride and Jesus as the bridegroom runs throughout the New Testament. To this day I have not known anyone who met someone, fell utterly in love, and then married that person all in the space of fifteen minutes.

Such a notion of marriage sounds silly to us, but that picture is not too different from what we have assumed in much of our evangelistic efforts.

Each Christian holds what I call an "evangelism equation," a particular view regarding how a person comes to know Jesus personally. This equation greatly influences how we seek to lead people to Christ. As a traditional "soul winner," my evangelism equation went like this:

Telling *the Message* + Call *to Response* =
Traditional Evangelism

This equation typifies most tracts and gospel messages in our day. Our emphasis has clearly been upon telling the gospel to unbelievers. Evangelicals especially have believed that if we can tell the gospel more clearly, then we will be more effective. A brief examination of any number of popular books on evangelism would reflect this strong emphasis on the message aspect of evangelism. I believe we have gotten the story partly right, but by and large have oversimplified the process of leading others to Christ.

The greatest shortfall of this approach is that it cuts out one of our strongest weapons as Christians: the kindness of God. It is one thing to tell the gospel and quite another to communicate, in a meaningful way, the love of God. Telling does not necessarily bring understanding. And telling is not welcomed until hearts are hungry.

I recently drove by a large evangelical church displaying this sign out front: *God loves you and wants to know you. There, now you can't say later on that you didn't hear it.* This statement is perhaps a little more rugged than what most of us are used to, but we have all been guilty of sending the gospel to others rather than bringing it as Jesus did, from individual to individual and from heart to heart.

Evangelism messages often apply pressure by quoting from 2 Corinthians 6:2: "Now is the day of salvation." Now is the day of salvation *if* that happens to agree with God's timetable for that particular person. What is the Spirit of the Lord doing in the hearts of those we encounter? As Jesus said, "No one can come to me unless the Father who sent me draws him" (Jn 6:44, RSV). Applying human pressure to someone is likely to do more harm than good. I no longer expect that each person I encounter will necessarily agree with the gospel, repent, and ask Jesus into his or her heart on the spot. I do, however, expect that something significant is taking place in people's hearts, whether they accept Christ at that moment or not.

Our aim has been to make evangelism a part of everything we do. We now see people come into a relationship with Christ in many of our groups and at all of our Sunday meetings—whether we do an altar call or not. People are coming to Christ in the parking lot, in the restrooms, in the hallways, and usually at the most unpredictable times. We've found that where a spirit of evangelism is welcomed, people come to Christ whether evangelism programs are going on or not.

At our Sunday morning meetings we seek to touch people with God's love in a variety of ways, beginning the moment they drive into our parking lot. To do this we have parking lot greeters who wear huge sponge hands like those you might see at a football game. These wavers welcome people as they arrive. To date we know of two people who have come to know Christ because of this simple act of welcome. One woman kept driving by on Sunday mornings wondering what kind of church would have wavers stationed in the parking lot. Curiosity got the better of her and she finally stopped in. After several visits, she accepted Jesus into her heart.

From the beginning, our aspiration has been to launch a style of evangelism that would become part of our everyday lives. Servant evangelism has accomplished just that. Extending God's love to others in practical ways has been the key in allowing us to reach people who live in our community. We have discovered over and over that as we come with a heart to serve people—instead of a heart to tell, preach, or talk down to them—they are very receptive.

*More people than ever are hungry for God.
But if we come to unbelievers with a message of
"Get right with God or get left,"
we are forcing them in or out.*

Over the last several years of doing servant evangelism, thousands of seeds of service and love have gone out around the city of Cincinnati. With each act of service, someone's life has been touched—someone who usually goes on to tell others about what was done for them in the name of the Lord. In short, when we have touched the lives of people where they *really live*—by lessening their pain and making their day a little more livable—those people who have been served go on to become walking advertisements for the kingdom of God and for the local church.

I read about a beer company which sponsored a contest to promote summer sales. Certain cans were specially rigged so that opening them triggered a recorded message: "You won!" When we serve others with hearts of love, a little voice is spoken by the Holy Spirit to those we serve: "You are loved! God is real! Come to me!" Much more than simply being served or receiving something for free, unbelievers experience the presence of God. By receiving the act of love we offer, they unknowingly are inviting the presence of God into their lives. Their hearts are being invaded.

More people than ever are hungry for God. But if we come to unbelievers with a message of "Get right with God or get left," we are forcing them in or out. While they may need to come into the kingdom, it may take some time to make the transition. Too often we try to make people decide for or against the Lord far too early in the process. What we immediately chalk up as a "rejection" of the gospel often should be scored as "incomplete."

Certainly, there is a time and place for a verbal presentation of the gospel. As Paul says, "How shall they hear without a preacher?" (Rom 10:14). Nevertheless, I believe we have reversed the natural order of evangelism. We need to love with our actions first, and then offer words of love to explain precisely what God's life is all about. Of course we must bring the message of the good news, but confining that message to words alone is a huge mistake. St. Francis said it best, "Wherever you go, preach the gospel, and if necessary, use words."

5. FOCUS ON PLANTING, NOT HARVESTING

A woman named Michelle Brandes was led to the Lord by Christian author Keith Green and went on to serve as his secretary for several years. Considering Michelle's background, this was a strange turn of events for her life. Raised in a Reformed

Jewish home in the San Fernando Valley area of Los Angeles, she would have qualified as a "God-fearer," although she had no personal relationship with Jesus.

Keith and his wife Melody befriended Michelle until finally one day she invited Jesus Christ into her heart. That would make a great ending to this story, except that nothing apparently happened when Michelle uttered that prayer. Over a period of more than two years, Keith led Michelle in a prayer of repentance an amazing six times!

Some might ask, "Why pray the same prayer so many times when only once is necessary to get through to God?" Keith shared the same basic explanation of the gospel each time, and Michelle prayed the same heartfelt and sincere prayer, but for some reason it didn't "take" until they prayed on the seventh occasion.

Most of the Christians I know would have taken Michelle back to the Scriptures and encouraged her to just believe the truth of God's Word. To quote a famous tract, she should get the train of "fact-faith-feeling" aligned properly. Keith was either smart enough or instinctive enough to keep asking Michelle to pray one more time until somehow she and the Lord got aligned. When in doubt, he kept on planting seeds of faith and love. Most importantly, Keith realized that God is the one doing the real work of evangelism. As we faithfully conduct ourselves as seed planters and waterers, God will complete the work of harvesting.

Planting a seed, not closing a deal. From a parallel reading of Acts and 1 Corinthians, I believe Paul had his own Howard Beale experience in Athens. Though he was one of the best educated men of his generation, Paul's trust in his intellect came to a screeching halt one day. According to the account in Acts 17, this famous apostle reasoned with the rich and famous and well-bred intellectual set of Athens.

Paul's track record was impressive. When this man spoke, things usually happened. Yet Luke describes the less than enthusiastic response to Paul's preaching on this particular day: "Paul departed ... however, some men joined him and believed"

(Acts 17:33-34). A few is better than none, but Paul was not used to such a meager response. As he left Athens for Corinth, this great preacher was shaken to the core by his experience. Later he wrote, "I was with you in weakness, in fear, and in much trembling" (1 Cor 2:3).

After this experience, Paul's entire view of evangelism changed. We all have ideas of what we think will work, but we don't find out what really works until we step out to do it. Paul no longer put his trust in finely crafted words. He said, "My speech and my preaching were not with persuasive words of human wisdom, but in demonstration of the Spirit and of power" (1 Cor 2:4). Never again would Paul minister with words of persuasion apart from utter dependence on the power of the Holy Spirit for his success in ministry.

Paul now clearly perceived an important truth: only the Holy Spirit can bring a person to faith. He goes on to make it clear that evangelism is a process: "I have planted, Apollos watered, but God gave the increase. So then neither he who plants is anything, nor he who waters, but God who gives the increase" (1 Cor 3:6-7). Human beings can play an important role in bringing the good news to others, but it is God alone who is the real evangelist.

When we talk about evangelism, we aren't generally talking about the planting-watering-harvesting cycle that Paul describes. We usually mean the results—the harvest alone. In fact, we have become so completely preoccupied with this last phase of the evangelism process that it has tainted our approach to bringing people to Christ. Sometimes I hear comments like,

"How many prayed the prayer?"
"How many were baptized?"
"How many responded?"
"How many did you close the deal with?"

When I would pray with someone to accept Christ, I used to say that "I led the person to the Lord." I no longer use that phrase because it is inaccurate. We need to understand that we are incapable of leading anyone to Christ whom the Holy Spirit is not already drawing.

Evangelism is a process that begins with planting along the lines of what Paul did. He and others like him would come into towns "not building on other men's work" and speak the basics of the life and gospel of Jesus Christ. Some would listen, some wouldn't. The process continued with the ministry of people like Apollos who watered and nurtured the already planted seed. At some point God himself would eventually reap a harvest as someone came to faith in Jesus Christ.

This concept flies in the face of our cultural value for an immediate conclusion. Americans don't tend to value process. At best, we tolerate any delay of gratification. We like closure. We are into results. Our houses are full of products that give testimony to our demand for immediacy and convenience: microwave ovens, remote controls to cable TV with umpteen channels, instant glue that forms a permanent bond in less than a minute.

I fear our cultural values of instant response and the bottom line have produced a distinctly American form of evangelism.

My last experience in purchasing a car wasn't too different from our typical American approach to evangelism. The salesman turned up the hype and twisted my arm with "for tonight, and tonight only, you can buy this car at this price. But as soon as you walk out the door, that offer is over. And please, if you don't buy tonight, don't tell my boss how ridiculously low I'm going on this vehicle. I could lose my job for giving you such an amazing deal."

I told him that I wasn't interested in buying anything without thinking it over, looking at our budget, and talking at length with my wife. She wouldn't be happy if I bought a car without consulting her, regardless of the "amazing deal" he was offering me. The salesman was desperate to close the deal while I was still in an information-gathering phase.

No sales manager gets excited when one of his struggling salespeople reports, "Well, I didn't make any actual sales this month, but I talked to a lot of people who are considering buying from us in the future." The typical response would be, "Who cares about *considering* buying from us. I want some closed deals and I want them now!"

I fear our cultural values of instant response and the bottom line have produced a distinctly American form of evangelism. When was the last time you heard someone get excited about planting seeds of God's love? Our evangelistic efforts are too often met with the question, "So, how many people prayed to accept Christ?" If the number is low we automatically feel disappointed and mutter, "Oh well, I tried."

That attitude is far from the one Paul took. Though he saw some people immediately accept Christ, the general response to Paul's message in Athens was lackluster. If he evaluated the fruit of his ministry on the response of that particular day, he probably would have given up early on. Fortunately Paul was able to see evangelism as a process—one which God himself is overseeing in each case. Paul also recognized his own vital and distinct role, even if he didn't get to see each planted seed come to fullness of faith.

C.S. Lewis, in his autobiography, *Surprised by Joy*, tells of struggling for months with the gospel. Somehow he couldn't get past the "unreasonableness" of the message. His story seems to me not too different from that of another famous British intellect, Bertrand Russell. Both of these men asked the same questions and came up with the same unsatisfactory answers early in life. Both describe a tremendous struggle with the gospel, of how they got into the issues of the gospel, dissected them point by point, but still could not come to belief. Though they asked many of the same questions, their conclusions were very different. Russell wrote of his struggle and conclusion that God is not real in his book *Why I Am Not a Christian*.

Lewis' story took a significant turn one day, almost to his surprise. The arena for battle shifted from Lewis' head to his heart. As he tells it, he was on the back of his brother's motorcycle on his way to the zoo. He says, "All that I know is that when I got on that motorcycle I did not believe in Jesus and that by the time we arrived at the zoo I was a believer."[4] When we rightly understand evangelism, we recognize that it is both a miracle and a mystery how any of us come to know Christ.

I personally saw a man whose heart was opened to the good news of Jesus Christ after it had been softened by the kindness of God. This happened when I was in Las Vegas doing an evangelism seminar. Typically when I speak at a conference for a couple of evenings, I also organize several outreaches into the community. After hearing about evangelism we always need to go one step further and actually do it!

On this particular Saturday, we put together a free Coke giveaway and washed windshields at several locations around town. At Sunday services on the following day, a young guy in his midtwenties walked into the meeting carefully carrying an empty Coke can. He had a somewhat glazed look on his face. One of the regulars went over to meet him and offered to throw away the can for him.

"Oh no, I'm not going to throw away this can. I'm saving this can. You see, *this* is the can of Coke that the Christians gave me yesterday in order to *show me God's love.*"

I don't know that man's full story, but it is clear that the simple act of giving away a cold drink at a stoplight in a conversation that only lasted ten seconds had made a significant impact on him. I believe that this man came much closer to having a relationship with Christ as a result of the kindness showed him. I don't know whether he accepted Christ that Sunday, but I do believe that he is well on his way toward knowing Christ in a personal and dynamic way. Even though I am the writer of this book, I am not the author of this man's story. Only God knows how his story is going to end.

Several years ago I would have been disappointed that I was

not able to "close the deal" with this man, that he had slipped away. I would have felt somewhat guilty that I didn't get him to pray the sinner's prayer right there at the meeting. I don't feel that pressure anymore because I know God himself is overseeing this process, not me. It was obvious this man has a heart inclined toward God. As long as he is asking the right questions, it's probably just a matter of time until he makes a commitment to Christ.

When we rightly understand evangelism, we recognize that it is both a miracle and a mystery how any of us come to know Christ.

♦♦♦

Am I disappointed when people don't respond? Hardly ever, because I know from lots of experiences that each person I meet is being worked on by the drawing power of the Holy Spirit. My joyful task is simply to bump them forward a notch or two through practical acts of love and service.

6

READY, *FIRE*, AIM!

"A knowledge of the path cannot be substituted for putting one foot in front of the other."
—M.C. Richards

"Give light, and the darkness will disappear of itself."
—Erasmus

WHEN I FIRST CAME TO Cincinnati I started getting together with several other men every Saturday for breakfast. Eventually our group added a Bible study. Our coziness was disrupted one week when the designated leader chose the topic of God's love for the poor as portrayed by the Minor Prophets. These inspired authors connect the coming of God's presence with his people stepping out to meet the needs of those who are hurting.

We desperately wanted to see God's presence in our midst, so we decided to make a leap of faith. Taking our Bible study one step further into a "Bible do," we began to put into practice God's written love for people by reaching out to those in need.

Our men's group would typically eat breakfast, do a brief Bible study, and then go out to do ministry. That began a tradition in our church of using Saturday mornings as a time for giving of ourselves to serve others in a practical way.

Our commitment to "Bible do's" forced us to move from theory to practice in our Christian lives. We will never be truly ready. We will forever be growing in our knowledge of how to evangelize more effectively, but we mustn't stipulate that our training process be complete before we begin to obey the Lord. If we wait until we have full understanding, we will never get out of the starting block.

Our commitment to "Bible do's" forced us to move from theory to practice in our Christian lives.

Our motto for several years has been, "Ready, *Fire,* Aim!" I have heard critics say, "That sounds reckless." Perhaps. Nevertheless, I vote to just get started—whether we feel ready or not. In my many years as a pastor I have seen too many Christians remain in the preparation mode without ever putting into action what they've been preparing to do. I heard Billy Graham once say at a crusade, "God has a difficult time guiding a rocket before it is launched. Get off the launching pad and guidance will come to you." Let's take a closer look in this chapter at the practicalities of launching out into servant evangelism.

PLAN, BUT PLAN AS YOU GO

I'm amazed at the number of people who come up to me at conferences and ask, "But how do you actually just start doing this?"

I usually respond by asking another question: "What's so difficult about cleaning a windshield? I can show you my technique, then you need to get out there and do it." The basic idea behind these servant evangelism projects is very simple. It's not that difficult to begin loving people in practical ways. We need to avoid the human tendency to make things overly complicated.

We often use planning as an excuse for not doing. Many times we're just waiting for someone to invite us into the game or waiting for someone in authority to give us permission to serve others in Jesus' name. It seems to me that permission has already been granted numerous times by Jesus and by those inspired by the Holy Spirit to write his words in Scripture.

I'm not against planning in the least. The Bible specifically tells us that "we should make plans ... counting on God to direct us" (Prv 16:9). We also read, "A prudent man foresees the difficulties ahead and prepares for them" (Prv 22:3). But we often take such caution too far in order to avoid taking risks. In many respects the church seems to prefer being expert *planners* rather than expert *doers.* That's why I say, "Plan as you go." Plan to the extent necessary, but don't go overboard.

While planning at its worst can be a crutch for not doing, a lack of planning will result in frustration and inefficiency for all concerned. Clearly we need to balance planning with the execution of those plans. The leadership in our church plans out events for a quarter of the year at a time. Our plans keep us on track and honest, but the key is always sticking to those plans as much as possible.

Start simple. Begin by working on projects that are inexpensive and don't require a lot of preparation time. Appendix one lists about seventy projects which we have used with some degree of success. With your own resources in mind, look for the ones which would be the easiest to accomplish without much preparation.

Just last week a local food chain donated one thousand cartons of eggs to our church. We had never given away eggs, but figured that most people eat them, so we planned to give them away door-to-door as a service project. Several small groups went into the community and gave one or two dozen eggs to each household. Two people said, "Funny you should stop by with eggs! I was just on my way out the door to buy eggs."

It doesn't take a lot of organization to pull off a successful project. Something as simple as eggs and eager people willing to knock on a few doors can make a huge impact on your community. Start with very simple projects with few moving parts. Later, after you've gotten some successes under your belt, you can tackle the more complicated ones.

Something is always better than nothing, but ideally when you launch out into servant evangelism, do several projects in quick succession to get your feet wet. If I had six people going out, I would choose two different projects right off that didn't require a lot of people power.

As you continue to gain experience, lots of different kinds of projects need to be available. Outreach is sort of like fishing. Fish bite in every kind of weather depending on the bait you use and the kind of fish you want to catch. Some sort of "catch" needs to be happening when you go out to do ministry. On a given day split up into three groups with an attitude of "We'll catch something if we try several approaches." If washing windshields doesn't work for some reason, maybe feeding parking meters will go over. If neither of those work, try cleaning toilets.

IDENTIFY THE PAINS OF YOUR CITY

God knows the hearts and needs of your community. Ask him to reveal those specific needs to you as you step out to serve. He promises to reveal himself to us if we seek him: "Call to me, and I will answer you, and show you great and mighty things, which you do not know" (Jer 33:3).

A huge key to success in reaching out to your city is having a grasp on local pressure points. What proves to be an effective outreach project in Seattle may not work so well in Omaha. Fortunately, God cherishes the people of both places and is perfectly capable of showing us how we can creatively enter their lives. The very best and most creative outreach projects for your community are ones that you will probably discover as you do service projects.

We live in a needy world. Their need is our open door for touching their hearts. The question is simply, "Given our present resources and boundaries, what could we do to touch these people with God's kingdom in a practical way?" God has more creative ideas than we could exhaust in a million lifetimes of ministry. Tap into his mind and take notes.

One way to receive God's guidance involves simply looking around you. Each person struggles with the pain of life. Ultimately all human pain stems from our alienation from God, but some types are unique to specific communities. In what specific ways do those who live in your city need help, healing, and wholeness? As we discover those particular needs and begin to meet them, we quickly gain credibility and a receptive audience.

For the past couple of years mail carriers from the north side of Cincinnati have been using our church parking lot as a spot for coffee breaks. One day another pastor and I went out washing windshields and decided to wash the windows of the mail truck parked at the edge of our lot. The carrier instantly opened up with us by asking if we would pray for his mother who has terminal brain cancer. We were able to interact at a deeper level in that five-minute conversation than we would have over years of passing him and saying, "Hi ... Bye."

Some of my best ideas for outreach projects have come to me as I strolled through the local mall with a cup of coffee in my hand and simply watched those who passed by.

When I first came to Christ I was much more sensitive to the pain of life around me because I too was hurting. After years of soaking up God's abundant love and healing, I began to not notice others' pain so much. I became a lot like the priest and Levite who passed by the man in the ditch. I could see with my eyes but yet walk right past and not take to heart the trauma of those in need. As we seek to reach out to our communities, it's time we noticed that pain once again.

How do you identify the pain of the people in your city? If you have no idea where to begin, simply spend a couple of hours walking around a local mall. Look into the eyes of those who pass by. Ask yourself and God, "How do they hurt? What could I realistically do to relieve some of the difficulties they're experiencing?" I believe you will receive new insights.

Some of my best ideas for outreach projects have come to me as I strolled through the local mall with a cup of coffee in my hand and simply watched those who passed by. They all have a bundle of needs. A popular cartoon captures the current predicament of most people. One woman tells a coworker, "Most of the people I know are on the verge of hysteria twenty-four hours a day, and they're the lucky ones. Everyone else *is* hysterical all the time."

Consider actually asking people at the mall their opinion. You could introduce yourself and say, "I'm a Christian. I want to do something practical for the people of this community. What do you think I could do?" I have also posed this same question in another way: "If Jesus Christ were here today and offered to help you, what would you ask of him?" You will have some enlightening conversations on your hands!

WHEN STARTING OUT, PAY YOUR OWN WAY AS MUCH AS POSSIBLE

I'm often asked, "How do you pay for these outreach projects?" From the beginning, our local fellowship has assigned 15 percent of its total income to evangelism and ministry to the poor. For an established church which hasn't had an outreach fund, this idea may seem impractical. Yet if the church holds evangelism as a value, eventually we must assign money to express that value. I challenge pastors to become financially committed to reaching out to those outside the church, but I realize that it takes time to go from zero percent of a budget to a significant allowance.

If you have no funds for getting started, consider pooling a bit of your own money. If you're in a small group, put your money together and invest in some supplies. With just ten dollars you can buy a couple of good squeegees, some Windex, and you're on your way! Perhaps it would be appropriate to put on a fundraiser to gather funds for purchasing equipment. Maybe the local mission fund could be tapped into. After all, this certainly qualifies as local missions!

Most of the projects we do in servant evangelism are actually very affordable. Sometimes for literally just a few dollars many people can be touched in a practical way. For example, one project we like to do is going door to door with sixty-watt light bulbs and offering to replace any burned-out ones. When purchased in bulk, light bulbs cost very little yet provide an entry point into the lives of each family.

REPORT TO YOUR PASTORS, BUT DON'T PUT EXPECTATIONS UPON THEM

I encourage you to take the slow route in getting your pastor involved in servant evangelism. Most pastors I know are already overextended. The best way to get their positive attention is to do a couple of projects on your own and then report back to them with your results. Pastors are always looking for a workable approach which can get the average person involved in evangelism. Although no long-term outreach program will be established without some sort of pastoral leadership, your personal enthusiasm for these projects needs to be shared with patience, wisdom, and tact.

After pastoring for tenty-two years now, I know that the spontaneous direction of my responsibilities revolves around reacting to internal problems. Evangelism falls under the category of "*pro*action" rather than "*re*action." At least in a small and perhaps symbolic way, I believe that pastors need to get out into the community on a regular basis. If we don't schedule these ventures into our busy lives, we will simply cave in to the pressures of day-to-day church life and perpetuate an unhealthy pattern of inwardness.

My own informal surveys indicate that less than 5 percent of pastors consistently spend time around the nonchurched. Servant evangelism provides necessary reality therapy because it gets them out into the real world. Besides, ultimately Christians will do only what their pastors do. I require all of the staff members of our church to participate in some sort of evangelism outing at least once per month. I also require all pastors on our staff to go out every other week. We're all very busy and could easily justify not doing so, but then we could easily get stuck in a little circle chasing our own tails.

*This pastor broke down weeping
while describing his experience. "I talked to
more unchurched people today than
I have in the past several years combined."*

A pastor in downtown Denver told me about his experience of putting on a Matthew's Party for the needy. Church members fed people, played games, led square dancing, and had a wonderful time. This pastor had even arranged for several of the players from the Denver Nuggets basketball team to take part. After the party had ended, they tallied up well over a thousand people who had attended.

This pastor broke down weeping while describing his experience. "I talked to more unchurched people today than I have in the past several years combined." Pastors obviously have a deep love for non-Christians, but the *ministry* of pastoring can easily separate and isolate them. We must resist the trend of giving aid to fellow believers and yet never spending time with people outside of our local fellowships.

ADDING WORDS TO YOUR DEEDS

What we say to explain our actions in servant evangelism is obviously of great importance. Since we put most of the stress on the deed being done, the few words we share ought to be carefully considered. This is the basic phrase we use to explain ourselves:

"We're doing a free community service project to show God's love in a practical way."

As I have already mentioned, the simple word "free" holds great power. Unfortunately, most of the time it is used with some sort of catch. When the church youth group offers a "free car wash," they really mean, "Donations are gladly accepted!" Door-to-door projects often elicit a jaded look from those who answer. "Yeah, right, I'm sure it's free ... so what do you want from me?" When we reassure them that there's no catch, that we are serving just for the joy of serving and showing God's love, people are often blown away! "You mean to tell me this is really free?"

When we use the important phrase "community service project," we are putting ourselves in the same league as the Kiwanis, Lions Club, and Boy Scouts. I don't consider this to be any sort of subterfuge. We are truly serving the community as we reach out in servant evangelism.

"Showing God's love in a practical way" is the evangelistic clause in our explanation. We have found this pregnant phrase especially effective in getting our foot in the door of the lives and hearts of those we serve. I have also found it fairly easy to go from those few words to a more in-depth conversation regarding Christ.

I encourage you to use this phrase exactly as I have shared it, at least when starting out in servant evangelism. Of course, you may find more effective ways of communicating this same message as you go along. Regardless of the phrase you use, it's important that you say a lot with just a few words. Remember, our goal is to encounter a lot of ships passing in the night while leaving them with something to think about afterward.

COMMIT YOURSELF TO A MINIMUM OF SIX MONTHS OF DOING PROJECTS

It takes time to see the results of servant evangelism. I recommend that you not seriously evaluate your results until you have been doing such projects for six months. The common tendency is to begin reaching out and then to immediately evaluate the daylights out of the little bit of practice we've gotten.

On the other hand, I do recommend that you keep track of the numbers of people you serve from week to week. This record will be a helpful motivator when it seems as though you're not making any headway. We can rejoice periodically with the thought, *With this many being served, surely some significant seeds are being planted in hearts through us.* We don't want to get stuck in a numbers game of notching our Bibles for each person we evangelize, but we do have to maintain our motivation and enthusiasm.

I encourage you to make it your goal to create an "atmosphere of evangelism" more than to run a program. Building such an atmosphere will take time. Good things will be sown from your first outing, but it will take time to begin to see the fruit of your labor. Typically it takes six months for a local church to catch on to this new approach to evangelism.

COULD I ASK YOU A QUESTION?

People who are initially exploring this idea of servant evangelism usually have a lot of questions. The following are a sampling of the ones I commonly hear. Hopefully they will address some of your concerns.

What's so different about servant evangelism? In a nutshell, the uniqueness of this approach to sharing the good news can be described in this way:

1. It's quick.
2. It's high volume.
3. It's done in groups.
4. It's culture-current.
5. It gives the Holy Spirit an open door to convict those we are leading to Christ.
6. It allows shy people to launch into effective evangelism.
7. It's an approach which Christian families can do together.
8. It's easily picked up by new Christians.
9. It's simple.
10. It's friendly, non-pushy, nonaggressive.
11. It appeals to every segment of our cities by providing many specific projects from which to choose.
12. It's emotionally safe for those who have been traumatized by negative experiences with evangelism.
13. It's giving-centered rather than asking-centered.
14. It provides a safe place for ambitious people to expend their energy.
15. It provides an open door for the miraculous—if God so moves.
16. It's big fun!

How does servant evangelism fit in with other approaches? God is ultimately overseeing the process of evangelism in each person's life. We are the seed flingers; he is the Master Gardener. God uses numerous connections to bring new children into his family. I am continually amazed at the diverse stories of conversion I hear from new believers.

Every person is at a unique place in their gradual awakening to the love of Christ. Servant evangelism draws everyone it touches closer to accepting Christ regardless of their own personal situation. In some cases we will be making initial contact with people who have never interacted with a Christian. At other times we will be watering the seeds already sown by others.

By itself, servant evangelism is incomplete
as an approach to sharing the gospel.
Traditional approaches alone are also incomplete.

◆◆◆

By itself, servant evangelism is incomplete as an approach to sharing the gospel. Traditional approaches alone are also incomplete. By focusing on the earlier phases of planting and watering, deeds of kindness tenderize hearts so they can later receive the message of God's love. I don't believe servant evangelism will work unless we also use more traditional approaches to actually harvest those accepting Christ. As we serve people, God will provide opportunities to explain the gospel message and eventually pray a sinner's prayer with someone. Many useful aids have been developed for this purpose, including *Evangelism Explosion,* the *Four Spiritual Laws,* and *Steps to Peace with God.*

How do people respond when served? Our service projects usually draw some sort of response, often in the form of inquiries about our church. One of the most often asked questions is "How long do your services last?" Others who are looking for a Bible-based fellowship ask, "Does your church believe in the Bible?"

Other responses vary. People in a good mood tend to react with surprise and gratefulness. Big city people—who tend to be more skeptical—wonder what we're up to and what we want from them. They also tend to be in a hurry most of the time, so we need to gear our projects to their pace. We happen to touch just a small percentage of people while they're in an open frame of mind. These individuals sometimes will talk at length with us. When we've had a chance to openly chat with folks, it seems that about 5 percent are open to coming to Christ right there on the spot!

What are the most typical questions people ask?

> "Who are you people anyway?"
> "What are you selling?"
> "What's the name of your church?"
> "What time do you meet?"
> "How long do your services last?"
> "Can I make a donation?"
> "What do you believe?"
> "Are you the kind of Christians that believe in prayer?"

I find it interesting that we hear very few theological questions. Hardly ever does someone ask exactly what we believe.

Will people be frightened or offended? Responses vary greatly, but seldom do people get overtly upset with us. A friend of mine in New York City has been reaching out with servant evangelism projects for about a year now. He has washed literally thousands of windshields in arguably the world's least friendly city. To date he has received only one negative response, surprisingly from two women with a big Bible on the dashboard! They shooed him away before he could get a word in edgewise.

Use the word "free" with a big smile and almost all of the negative responses will be eliminated.

When people are frightened it is usually because they don't know how to respond to such an unusual offer. I have found the best way to put someone at ease is simply to put on the biggest smile you can muster. Smiles are incredibly disarming. Not long ago I was going from car to car washing windshields in a mall parking lot. I was about half finished with one car when I saw three big, college-aged guys running toward me. Their look of suspicion turned to laughter when I turned around smiling. They said they thought I might have been breaking into their car, then thanked me enthusiastically and went their way.

Simply making good eye contact is another helpful way to let people know that they have nothing to fear. Looking confident will also convince potential critics that we are OK. When any kind of tension develops, I find it very helpful to mention the word "free" as quickly as possible. Having been conditioned to requests for donations, people automatically expect us to ask for something in return for our service. Use the word "free" with a big smile and almost all of the negative responses will be eliminated. When we go door to door, residents are sometimes fearful to the point of not wanting to open their doors. They may yell, "Who is it?" through the closed door. Usually I yell back, "I'm Steve. We're giving away great free stuff." That usually overcomes their resistance.

What negative responses do you get? We usually seek the minimal amount of permission when doing projects. When it seems appropriate we even wash windshields or plug parking meters of unattended cars. On occasion people will walk up as we are washing their windshield and say, "Hey, stay away from my car!" Usually they express appreciation once they hear our explanation.

Sometimes people assume that we're selling something. Especially in busy downtown areas where a lot of panhandlers are operating, many of those who pass by are afraid of making eye contact with a stranger. One of our small groups is comprised of business people who work in downtown Cincinnati. About once a month this group does some sort of outreach to other business people in a center section called Fountain Square. Usually they give away gourmet coffee, wash windshields, or clean toilets for area businesses. The group leader reports that they have gained increasing credibility from the usually skeptical business people as they have continued serving in these ways.

In any single project we find some measure of rejection to our offer to serve. Whether we are giving away Cokes or raking leaves or refilling bird feeders, some people give us a curt "no" with little explanation. We are not disappointed because we have consistently seen that the power of what we're doing isn't confined to the particular product or service we offer, but simply the idea that we are doing this to show God's love. That offer is so powerful that it really does unsettle people when they consider it.

For months we have been cleaning the front windows of an Ohio State liquor store. The manager's first response to our offer to wash his windows for free was, "Sure it's free this time, but how much will it be next time?" We've never taken money from anyone for any of our projects, and this man would be no exception. After five or six months of serving this man, we are now on a first-name basis. Recently he confided in us that he'd returned to the church he grew up in after being gone for several years—all because we had begun to serve him. Our offer was spurned at first, but the invitation had an eventual effect.

We realize before we even set foot outside of the church parking lot that a certain percentage of our seeds of kindness will be rejected.

When we clean toilets, we experience about a 50 percent rejection rate on our first offer. About the worst that happens is that we are denied permission, the usual reason being that the employee wants to check with the boss. Sometimes the person is so shocked that they don't know what to say. When we are denied permission we usually offer to come back some other time to do something practical. Then we make it a point to return to that same home or business a couple of weeks later. Usually we aren't turned down the second time around.

How do you deal with rejection? We realize before we even set foot outside of the church parking lot that a certain percentage of our seeds of kindness will be rejected. Some people will say no to about anything offered them in life. I have met certain people who seem to walk through life with a big NO written across their faces.

Surfers describe a wave that is almost too rough to ride as being "gnarly." I have discovered that a certain percentage of the population goes through life with a consistently gnarly attitude. These folks are mad most of the time. Those who do reject our offer are usually mad before we ever talk to them. If we were giving out fifty dollar bills as a servant evangelism project, they would probably reject our offer. Even these people are being worked on by the grace of God, but they probably aren't ripe for harvesting.

One summer, on a hot Friday afternoon, we were giving away soft drinks to motorists on their way home from work. One woman was furious at us for approaching her car at all. She yelled, "How dare you offer me a drink! I'm calling the police as soon as I get home because I know for certain this is illegal." Apparently she was having a rough day. We did nothing to irritate her; she didn't even know who we were and yet she was mad at us.

We didn't allow this woman's rejection to stop us or even to slow us down. We continued on to the next driver with as big a smile as we could muster. Coincidentally, the next car happened to be a police cruiser. He gladly took a diet drink, thanked us, and commented, "This project is a wonderful idea. More churches ought to do this sort of thing."

In short, we don't take rejection personally. We aren't spending enough time with people or doing anything to elicit rejection. They don't even know us, so how can they be rejecting *us*? If they do refuse, they're actually rejecting the offer of kindness. Our job as bringers of God's kingdom is to find the people who are open and invite them into God's family. With those who aren't ready to respond, we just smile and keep going. The important point to remember is that we can't let a negative response scare us away from the next person—someone who is likely to be more open.

It's impossible to know what's going on inside of those with whom we interact, but I have a theory about those who go ballistic at our offer. I believe that many people in this category are being worked on by the power of the Holy Spirit, and that we happen to be one more point along the way before they finally come into a relationship with Jesus Christ. Somehow, our presence as representatives of God irritates them and they react in anger. Paul the apostle, for example, was his most violent just before his conversion on the road to Damascus (Acts 9:1-9).

We need to trust that God will redeem every episode of rejection. Don't forget the inherent power of the offer we are making. We recently had a crew cleaning toilets in a local mall. At one store the employee running the cash register said, "I don't know if you should. It's probably OK, but I'd better ask the boss first. Please come back next Saturday." When the team returned the following week the employee reported that not only was the owner willing to let our team clean, but that when the boss heard that we had come to clean the toilets, he began to openly weep. This employee admitted, "I've never seen him get emotional or anything. He was really touched by your offer to help us!"

What activities don't work well? We've had our share of failures. We view each mistake as an opportunity to grow in our effectiveness as servants. Most of our failures are actually great ideas that just need a little adjustment or fine-tuning. Here are some of the more creative failures we've experienced:

- *Accidently filling a radiator with windshield washing fluid.* The washer reservoir looks a lot like the radiator reservoir! We paid the fifty dollars to have the woman's radiator flushed.

- *Washing the windshield of an already clean car.* We later paid to have the car washed again.

- *Washing the windshield of a car with a couple of dogs inside.* The dogs were hyperactive and went berserk, doing some damage to the interior. We agreed to pay for damages, but the owner never followed up on our offer.

- *Accidently setting off car alarms.* Sometimes a sensitive alarm will go off when we lift a wiper to clean the windshield. Even though this has happened dozens of times, we've had only one negative encounter with a man who appeared to be in a big hurry and counted us as an inconvenience to his tight schedule. Typically when people come to check out what happened, they are relieved to see that we're simply there to serve them. We always look for stickers indicating a car alarm, but not all cars post such a warning. Our rule of thumb is to stay away from vehicles that appear to be newer or more expensive. To date we've never had the owner of an older car get angry at us for serving them!

This is an up-to-date list of our failures, but I fully expect that list to grow longer. If we aren't failing on a regular basis, then I assume that we aren't taking enough risks. A growing list of failure stories would indicate to me that we're in a place of balance between prudence and activism.

What are the immediate results of applying servant evangelism?

1. *Most importantly, non-Christians will begin to open their hearts to God's love.* People are a lot like porcupines: they either turn to us with their soft, vulnerable side or their prickly, skeptical side that says, "I don't want to hear anything about this Jesus you are talking about." A free car wash in New York City prompted one "porcupine" to turn his soft side to us. This man worked for the sanitation department.

When he drove into our car wash he was angry and disgusted because we had caused a traffic slowdown on his route.

The driver of the garbage truck shook his head and muttered, "When I get back to the garage, I just know the other guys aren't gonna believe this happened."

This emotionally charged encounter changed instantly when we offered to wash his entire garbage truck for free. Before he could say no we were eagerly serving him. This man stood in stunned silence just shaking his head. A couple of the girls standing by explained to him that we just wanted to show him God's love in a practical way. The driver of the garbage truck muttered, "When I get back to the garage I just know the other guys aren't gonna believe this happened." A few minutes later he asked for prayer for a number of issues in his life—right in the middle of the Big Apple's hustle and hurry.

2. *Christians will be built up in their courage to share their faith with unbelievers.* I've found that about 50 percent of Christians have shared their faith at some point, but only about twenty percent have actually prayed to lead someone to Christ. Servant evangelism serves as a type of "baby step" toward more risky approaches. As fearful Christians meet unbelievers in a safe, nonconfrontational setting where they experience success, they will gradually grow in their ability to tell others what Jesus has done for them.

What are the long-term results of doing servant evangelism?

1. *The church will become oriented toward action.* The church is in continual need of redefining. It seems clear that the

church in America is living in an age of great inwardness. This week I received a monthly catalog from one of the largest Christian book distributors in the country. Out of the one thousand titles, only five concerned evangelism and outreach. About two dozen books addressed the challenge of raising teenagers, about one hundred dealt with co-dependency issues, and about fifty discussed the end times.

In light of this inward focus, we need to ask the question, "Why does the church exist?" We certainly exist to worship God and to grow in wholeness and Christlikeness, but Jesus made it clear that we must also give of ourselves if we hope to keep growing. The Great Commission links God's special presence to the action of the church going into the world. "Go therefore and make disciples ... and lo, I am with you always" (Mt 28:19-20, RSV). God is with us in an immediate sense as we carry his life into the world.

Human nature always points the emotional compass inward. To be the church, we must on occasion grab that compass and point it outward. Jesus promised that "rivers of living water" would flow out of the hearts of all who believe in him. Try as we may, God will not bless any attempt to make a stagnant and cloistered pond of that river of life. As we bring the kingdom of God into the community, we will change the world in which we live.

2. *The church will be redefined to the surrounding community.* The church in general has taken a lot of blows over the last several years, especially in the wake of scandals involving sex and money. The world has falsely pictured the entire church as beggars always on the verge of going out of business. We've also been pegged as hucksters always looking to get something for nothing. The third picture the watching world has of the church is that of a monastery whose residents have only one message, "Come in and join us." The world isn't looking to be part of a failing cause. They want nothing to do with fast-talking, slick approaches.

As we begin to do humble acts of service in the community, we will restate our identity. Instead of separatists who are constantly judging the world, we must extend forgiveness, acceptance, and love from God. New definitions are slow to catch on, but hard work will get their attention. We become viable in the eyes of the world as we get beyond ourselves and serve our way into their hearts. In an age when the church has been judged by the world as being irrelevant and out of touch with people's very real needs and pains, we prove ourselves worthy of trust.

3. *The community will be saturated with the presence of these deeds of kindness.* The word "saturate" may seem like an odd word to use in reference to evangelism, but it seems to fit when you consider the long-term effect of this approach. Cincinnati may be an exception to the general rule, but it suggests the level of potential impact. We have been doing servant evangelism projects consistently for the past eight years, each year expanding our outreach. One year we directly touched about one hundred thousand people in greater Cincinnati. Add to that the other congregations in the city who are doing these outreaches and the total number touched was in the neighborhood of one hundred twenty thousand.

The 1993 population of the Cincinnati area was 1.75 million. That means we were approaching the point of touching one-tenth of the city each year. Of course, we encounter many people more than once during a year, but we are still touching a significant part of the city each year. As we continue to serve more and more people, we will be touching 10 or even 20 percent of the city per year. Over a several year period, we could touch huge numbers of the population.

Although our church membership numbers over two thousand, the lion's share of this work is being carried out by about two hundred people. A friend of mine has a church of about twelve hundred in a city of about one hundred thousand. His church is getting out into the community more and more with servant evangelism projects. In a few years, if they continue expanding, they could feasibly touch nearly the entire city each year with these high-impact deeds of kindness.

But aren't you really just using these service projects as a means for advertising your church to the community? I can honestly say that we aren't. Our outreach often leads to growth as a side benefit, but we would lose our integrity if growth was our reason for serving. Such an attitude would also rob the service of its power in people's lives. We aren't giving of ourselves to get anything. Even if we stopped growing altogether, we would continue to serve just as consistently. We must serve for the sake of our own spiritual health. Growth, which seems predictable, must be viewed as serendipity.

◆◆◆

We aren't giving of ourselves to get anything.
Even if we stopped growing altogether,
we would continue to serve just as consistently.

As we go about loving with no strings attached, God seems to attach a string of some sort to those actions. He seems to create a tie between the person we serve and himself. Our prayer in going out into the community has often been, "Oh God, let them forget us, but let them never forget you!"

As we serve with a good heart, God sends people to us—many of whom we've never served! A spiritual siphon draws people into our church. With very little advertising going on last year we had about five thousand people visit us, 60 percent of whom were unchurched. In summary, you might ask, "You mean that as we serve and *don't* go out of our way to make our church known in the community, that God is going to bring people to us anyway?" That's exactly what we have seen in Cincinnati.

NUTS AND BOLTS

"Charity is the bone shared with the dog when you are just as hungry as the dog."
—Jack London

W E SAW A REMARKABLE response to kindness not long ago at a Bengals football game. About twenty-five people from our fellowship met briefly in our church parking lot, prayed, and loaded up fifteen hundred cold cans of pop. They set up a table near one of the entrances to the stadium and simply began asking the fans, "Would you like diet or regular? This is to show you God's love in a practical way." The workers also slipped a small business card under the top with our phone number and name. (We consider this a very soft sell, just enough to give people a point of reference if they want to look us up.)

As the evangelism team was going about this project, a Cincinnati policeman who had been directing traffic walked up. I don't know if it was his uniform, the mirrored sunglasses, or his belt complete with a nightstick, but they felt intimidated and wondered what he was going to say. The policeman asked, "What are you doing?"

The team leaders responded cheerfully, "We're just giving away drinks to show God's love."

To that he asked, "Can I ask you a question? Could I have one?" Then this officer walked back to his post and carried on with directing traffic, but this time with a diet drink in his hand. To our utter surprise, he stopped some of the cars and pointed in our direction. "Do you see those people over there? They're giving away soft drinks to show God's love in a practical way."

This episode captures the essence of servant evangelism. Something in this man's heart told him, "This is an authentic group of people. They are speaking the truth." Though few words were exchanged, this policeman's heart was opened wide as we showed him love in the form of something as simple as a soft drink.

Even though this approach doesn't require a rocket scientist, it's so different from traditional programs that questions abound. We've learned many lessons in consistently doing servant evangelism over the last eighteen years. There are smart ways and not-so-smart ways of reaching out to our communities. In this chapter I want to share with you several troubleshooting tips, the "nuts and bolts" of doing these kinds of projects. These simple principles have helped us to effectively share the life of God with others.

PROVIDE A PLACE FOR EVERY LEVEL OF COMMITMENT

Leaders need to provide a lot of different options for becoming involved in servant evangelism. Some people can take on a large challenge, but we can expect most to only venture out occasionally. It is important to receive people at their level of readiness for doing ministry and to work with them where they actually are—not where we'd ideally like them to be.

I see people as being able to respond at four levels of commitment and challenge. A small percentage of folks are what I call the "Rambos" of evangelism because of their radical commitment and willingness to experiment in ministry. Out of over two thousand members in our church, I would classify about fifty as belonging in this category. These folks go out to do projects at least once every week regardless of the weather. While they don't reflect the norm, this is a good group for trying out new projects.

Not very many people can relate to the high cost of that level of outreach. We need to offer plenty of easy, entry-level projects for the bulk of believers. The more challenging projects are great and we ought not to get rid of them. The radicals thrive on the equivalent of a seven-foot high jump. On the other hand, we also need to offer a *six-inch* high jump for all those basic cowards who love Jesus. Our goal should be to provide outreach projects which can be done by the person with average gifting in evangelism.

Another group of people are the ones who go out monthly to do service projects. Still others participate in quarterly outreaches of some sort. Finally, we have a large number of people who buy in marginally to the practice of servant evangelism by doing some project on a yearly basis. I challenge people to get involved in servant evangelism about once a month. If we can get lots of people committed to going out once every four to six weeks, we will make a huge impact and no one will have to carry an undue burden. Small groups in particular seem to be able to respond to that level of frequency.

HAVE ALTERNATIVE PROJECTS SET UP IN CASE OF INCLEMENT WEATHER

We've been doing this long enough to know that Murphy's Law is real! ("Anything that can go wrong will go wrong at the worst possible moment!") While weather doesn't have to be a deterrent to our outreaches, we do need to be prepared for whatever the day may bring. Different weather just means that we will meet the needs of people in a slightly different way. If we had prepared to do a car wash and it ends up raining, we could just provide an umbrella escort at the local grocery store. If it's too cold to wash windshields, we could go door to door giving away light bulbs.

Don't lose heart in bad weather. *Do* be prepared. If you live in an area with predictably rainy weather—such as Seattle—you will need to develop a variety of rainy weather projects that reflect the needs of your community. In colder northern states and Canada, you will need to develop projects that work well with six months of snow and cold.

MINIMIZE FEARS OF PARTICIPANTS BY COMMUNICATING CLEARLY

1. *Establish clearly defined time parameters.* Clarify in advance how long you're going to be out. Making a commitment to participate in an outreach project is much easier if the time factor is made known up front. At the time of going out to do ministry, make it clear when everyone is to gather together to return home. Once you set a return time, stick to it. If you hope for quality workers to be involved with you, you'll need to be as clear as possible as to what will be expected of them each time they go out.

2. *Make use of a "coach" in projects requiring more than ten people.* Since we use our Bible study groups and home fellowships to do most of our servant evangelism outreaches, our small group leaders also serve as the evangelism leaders for their groups. Their main job is to guarantee that each participant has an outstanding time doing the outreach project. The coach serves as a combination "cheerleader" (moving about to see that people are enjoying themselves) and as a "go-fer" (going for this and that). Those who make a special effort to come out and serve should never run out of the necessary supplies. The coach will need to anticipate and then resolve any problems his or her team members may encounter.

WHAT ABOUT GETTING PERMISSION FOR PROJECTS?

We seem to be living in an age of litigation madness with law-suits being filed at the drop of a hat. Business owners are perhaps the most aware of this trend. I would recommend the following guidelines in terms of seeking permission.

1. *Ask for the minimum amount of permission for doing a project.* A Sam's warehouse store is located just down the street from our church building. We frequently visit their parking lot to do windshield washing. Over the last several years, I have never asked for permission to be on their property. I purposely start with cars in the employee parking area so that what we're doing is no secret.

   I suspect that if we were to actually ask permission, the official answer might be "No, you can't officially do that here because our insurance doesn't cover you." There isn't really a lot that can go wrong while washing windshields. Obviously we are there to *serve,* not to sue. Don't be paranoid. If you ask enough questions, you'll find the answer is going to be no to many of your requests to do outreach projects.

2. *Don't blatantly ignore common sense regarding getting permission. On the other hand, don't ask too many questions.* It's hard to say "always" or "never" in regard to seeking permission for projects. You'll just have to be guided by your intuition. For example, if I wanted to give away coffee inside a local mall, I would unquestionably seek permission from the mall management. However, if we were washing windshields outside in the parking lot, I might not ask for permission. At suburban grocery stores in Cincinnati, it's necessary to ask permission to give away coffee, but we regularly do this same project at an urban grocery store and never ask permission. No employee of that store has ever given us a second glance, even though we show up approximately every other Saturday morning.

3. *If you are denied permission to do a project at a promising location, offer to come back to service just the employees of that business.* I have found this a good door-opener in stubborn cases. Once the managers see that you're authentic, they will likely open the door for you to come back to serve their customers. Recently we were denied permission to wash windshields at the parking lot of a nationwide department store. We felt that this would be a great locale for doing servant evangelism, so we approached the manager again and offered to do a free car wash just for the store employees. He recognized our sincere enthusiasm and invited us back. I believe that we will be allowed to do other projects at that store in the near future.

4. *If you do encounter problems, don't forget that your smile is powerfully disarming to critics!* We rarely have any negative responses, but it is always prudent to have a strategy in case you do. Not long ago I was washing windshields in the parking lot of a mall. An employee came out excitedly saying, "Who do you think you are, washing windshields? You can't do this!"

My response was simply to smile. As mechanical as it may seem, a smile is a very powerful and disarming means for dealing with irate people. Then I explained what we were doing by saying, "This is a free community service project we're doing to show God's love." The employee immediately calmed down and said, "Well, if it's a community service project, I guess that's OK."

On another occasion while I was washing windshields by myself at a department store parking lot, a local rent-a-cop drove up to ask what I was doing. He had a look on his face that seemed to say, *I don't know what you're doing, but this better be good.* I put on my best smile and volunteered enthusiastically, "I'm doing a free community service project to show God's love." His look of suspicion changed to a simple, "Oh." Before long this officer was out of the car walking along with me. As I washed windshields, we talked about a variety of subjects and became virtual friends!

IF REASONABLE, RETURN TO THE SAME PLACES TO SERVE

We have been returning to a number of malls in the Cincinnati area for several years now. At first we found the management of these malls to be a bit skeptical. They naturally wondered what the catch was. Typically we were granted permission with several conditions attached. After going back to these same malls for years, we have gained great favor. In fact, in several cases, the malls now insist on paying for our supplies! One Christmas we were given five thousand dollars in wrapping paper at one mall. Another one gave us fifteen hundred dollars worth of Polaroid film for a photo outreach.

One Christmas we were given five thousand dollars in wrapping paper at one mall. Another one gave us fifteen hundred dollars worth of Polaroid film for a photo outreach.

When returning to the same locations, be sure you don't overextend your welcome. Being present too often at a particular place of business could be seen as a nuisance. In order to avoid impeding the flow of business, we make it a rule to be at a business for no more than one hour at a time. That means if we are going out for two hours of ministry, we generally stay at one location for about an hour, then move to a second locale. We want to avoid the appearance of "camping out" in front of any particular store. We also want business owners and managers to be glad to see us when we return the next time.

WHAT SAFETY AND LIABILITY ISSUES DO WE NEED TO CONSIDER?

1. *Wear bright orange vests or hats if you're going to be out in traffic.* It's better to be safe than sorry if you're serving around moving vehicles. Sometimes when we do projects people get distracted by what we're doing and end up not paying close attention to their driving. Bright is better.

2. *Go in teams of a minimum of two.* Pair veterans up with newcomers and insist that people stay together. Most of these projects are absolutely safe, but we still want to be sensitive to the fears of newcomers. Besides, it's biblical to go in pairs and it just makes good sense. When Jesus sent out the seventy he knew that the more experienced disciples could give faith to those who had never gone out before.

   Why two instead of more? Three or more seems to be intimidating, especially if they're all men. Some projects, such as washing cars, will require a larger group. But even in these projects, I recommend using small teams of two working together in order to impart ministry skills and to promote fellowship.

3. *Use name tags for team members.* We use name tags whenever they would lend a touch of legitimacy and professionalism. Their usefulness will vary depending on your targeted areas. In a skeptical, upper-middle-class suburb, name tags can give you an extra measure of credibility. They also give you the appearance of being part of something larger than yourself. Merchants will often feel better about letting you set up a display in their store areas. If you decide to use name tags, I recommend computer-generated, professional looking ones which include the name of the church, your logo, and the name of the individual who is serving.

4. *Use walkie-talkies.* When doing outreach projects we usually split up into small teams within the same general area. We aren't very far from one another, but we can't see each other. Walkie-talkies can be a helpful tool, especially in an urban area. Monitoring supplies and dealing with questions becomes much easier without having to track people down. Remember, one of the primary goals of each outing is to make sure each participant has a positive experience and leaves wanting to come back for the next one. (FM walkie-talkies cost under one hundred dollars per radio and can reach up to a mile.)

WHAT EQUIPMENT CONCERNS SHOULD WE CONSIDER?

1. *Use high-quality equipment.* The people you are serving will feel valued if you use high quality products. Conversely, the impact of your service can be compromised if you use inferior equipment. Often the difference between mediocre and excellent requires just a little bit more money and a little bit more effort.

2. *Learn to use your equipment properly.* None of the projects we commonly do requires an extreme measure of expertise, but some insightful training is needed in most. I always spend a few minutes covering the bases regarding each project before we set out.

   For example, washing windshields isn't very difficult, but if you aren't familiar with a squeegee you can easily streak the window. A well-cleaned windshield will be noticed by the driver. On the other hand, a streaked windshield is irritating and even worse than a dirty one. Before going out, newcomers need a short lesson on avoiding streaks.

   Certain projects make speed and efficiency more important. For example, the sheer number of cars pulling into a free car wash often creates a traffic jam. We need to do a superior job of serving people in our projects without adding extra hassle to their busy lives. The time spent in training and organization will increase the speed and quality in our services.

3. *Over-purchase supplies.* It is better to have leftover supplies than to run out when you're in the midst of an outreach. By running out of equipment or supplies, you're making a very negative statement to your workers: "We weren't expecting anything great to happen here today." A good rule of thumb is to have enough for that outreach plus the next one. You'll use the extras soon enough. Most of the supplies needed for our projects are inexpensive, so over-purchasing is typically more a matter of planning than finances.

4. *Establish an equipment closet.* There's no need to reinvent the wheel every time you go out to do servant evangelism. I know of nothing more irritating in doing projects than getting people gathered, sensing the Lord's presence and blessing, only to find a glitch in the area of equipment. I believe that it's important to have an ample supply of whatever you may need for a particular type of ministry.

Our closet consists of brooms, rakes, window squeegees, cases of soft drinks, ice chests, toilet cleaning kits, car washing equipment, light bulbs, batteries for smoke detectors, leaf blowers, etc. I want to create an atmosphere for those who gather to serve that we are equipped for come what may. I also want them to know that we can take on as many workers as show up. My hope is that those who go out this week to do ministry will feel enthusiastic enough to bring their friends next week.

BE SURE TO DO A QUALITY JOB

These free deeds of love make a powerful impression on those we serve—but only if we do a good job. The media often portrays Christians as being out of touch with fashion, current trends, and doing just enough to get by in life. This image is untrue and unfair, but we need to reckon with it just the same. If we do a bang-up, quality job, then we will go a long way toward tearing down these negative images.

We don't need to be neurotic perfectionists, but a reasonably good job is within reach of everyone.

If you are taking a role of leadership in servant evangelism projects, I recommend *The E Myth* by Michael Gerber. This book discusses the difficulty in maintaining quality services as projects and businesses grow. Both churches and businesses are often victims of their own success. Our initial success can yield more participants, but can also diminish the level of quality. We don't need to be neurotic perfectionists, but a reasonably good job is within reach of everyone.

Every once in a while we will get a phone call from a dissatisfied customer complaining that we did more harm than good in our attempt to serve. Recently someone complained that we smeared the window of his recently washed car. In cases like that we always offer to pay for a professional car wash. We're not discouraged by phone calls from irate people; instead, we just decide to do a better job on our next outing.

ALLOW TIME AFTER A PROJECT FOR PARTICIPANTS TO DOWNLOAD

I have found it helpful to have a debriefing time in the wake of ministry. We refer to this as a "do and tell" time. Now that we've done something, let's talk about it, compare notes, and let our hair down. This gives people the chance to bring to completion the process of learning. We truly learn what we can do, digest (information), and discuss. Jesus apparently did something similar when he received back the seventy after they had gone out to minister God's love to the surrounding towns and villages. They returned from their missions and shared lots of stories with one another.

We begin with *words* of training. We then do *works* of training as we put the theory into practice. And then we compare accounts with others who have stepped out along with us to give away God's life. Spirited discussions often follow ministry outings. After going out we usually gather at a fast food restaurant at a designated time. Over a taco and burrito the conversation may sound something like this:

"How did it go with you?"
"When you served people, did they seem open?"
"Which project did you enjoy the most?"
"What did you say or do differently that could help us to be more effective the next time we go out?"
"Where shall we go next time?"

Beginning anything new is a lot easier when we have a "loose grip" attitude. This is best achieved when our primary goal is to enjoy ourselves and just plain have fun with one another. Evangelism then becomes a by-product of our fun. A recent newcomer to servant evangelism recently confided in me, "You know, you can't pay to have this much fun in the world."

Record What You've Learned for Future Reference

Any energy spent in recording what you've learned after each outing will be well spent. Each time you'll gain insight into how to more effectively give away God's love. Notice what words seem to hit home, what products work the best, and how much of each product to bring along. Take note of which shopping areas are the most receptive to your outreach gestures and return there. You will notice a marked difference in the atmosphere and receptivity of certain stores and neighborhoods. Some are definitely more friendly and responsive than others.

Also, keep a log of how many people you are touching with various amounts of goods and services. Keeping a record of numbers can be helpful for both personal motivation and practical purposes like supply needs. Knowing trends can also help leaders to evaluate and plan for future growth.

Don't Be Concerned with the Immediate Return of Your Efforts

Resist the temptation to take your results too seriously. For every person we serve our experience has shown that two or three more are indirectly touched. Those we contact typically go on to tell others, "You wouldn't believe what just happened to me." We recently hosted a team of teenagers who did outreach for several weeks during the summer. These teens received basic training in a variety of ministry skills and then spent their afternoons going out into the community to do various outreach projects.

◆◆◆

I believe that much of the time we see only the tip of the iceberg of how our serving affects others.

At the end of their second week they were in need of a little pep talk to lift their spirits. Cincinnati's hot and humid summers can wear anyone down. We estimated that they had *directly* served six thousand people and *indirectly* touched another group of at least equal size by shock value alone. That meant that we had communicated God's love to twelve thousand people over the two-week period.

I believe that much of the time we see only the tip of the iceberg of how our serving affects others. Probably the best stories remain unknown to us. My guess is that we'll hear some of the conclusions to our projects when we get to heaven. I expect to meet a few folks who walk up and identify themselves as "I'm the guy you gave a cup of coffee to in downtown Cincinnati one time. That was the beginning of my coming to know Christ."

On a Friday afternoon when we were giving away cold drinks, a young man named Josh met an older woman as she came up to the stoplight. She said, "The last time you gave me a drink I cried all the way home. I realized that God loves me."

Josh quickly replied, "Well I guess you're gonna cry all the way home today, too. Here's your drink!"

PRAY BEFORE, PRAY DURING, AND PRAY AFTER

1. *Intercede for your projects.* Remember, servant evangelism involves "low-risk—high-grace" projects. It is very easy to underestimate the spiritual side of what is going on in people's hearts. We must remember that we are absolutely dependent upon the Lord's presence for fruitfulness. If God is upon these deeds of service, then those we touch will be drawn toward Christ. If the Holy Spirit isn't upon these works, then they aren't much more than nice but empty gestures.

   Our attitude must be, "If God shows up, something wonderful is going to happen here. If he doesn't, then we won't see much impact." Jesus tells us that his will is for us to bear fruit that will remain (Jn 15:16). Our fruit will remain as we depend on the presence and blessing of God for success in outreach projects.

2. *Pray as you serve.* As we are conducting these projects our prayers are usually simple, perhaps along these lines: "Come, Holy Spirit. Anoint this project. Use these simple acts of love to broadcast your reality and love to every single person we encounter today. Let them forget us, but remember you."

3. *Pray as you finish.* When you finish your outreach project, I recommend that you spend a few moments in prayer sealing your efforts before God. Tell the Lord that you are dependent upon him for lasting influence to occur in the lives you've touched. Ask the Holy Spirit to follow the people you've touched all the way home. Invite him to have his way in their lives.

4. *What about praying for people while doing serving projects?* You will be amazed at how many people are actually open to receiving prayer in public. It isn't always appropriate to pray—or even to offer to pray—for those we are serving. Sometimes though, it just fits. Our rule of thumb is this: *Be open to praying for people if they seem open to it.* We want them to invite us into their lives. We aren't coming on like gangbusters knocking down the door to their hearts.

◆◆◆

If you find yourself with someone who wants prayer, don't embarrass the person by doing something outlandish.... Be sensitive to where most people you'll encounter are spiritually. Don't lay hands on them; they won't understand.

◆◆◆

If you find yourself with someone who wants prayer, don't embarrass the person by doing something outlandish. Though you may be comfortable praying out loud or loudly, be sensitive to where most people are spiritually. Don't lay hands on them; they won't understand. Also, it's absolutely fine to pray a short prayer with your eyes open. When we do pray for folks, we usually ask them to contact us to let us know what happened in response to the prayer offered. Our hope is that people will begin to look for God's action in their lives as further evidence of his love for them.

A DELAYED REACTION

Jesus saw it as imperative that we conduct ourselves in the power of the love of God. His love flowing through our lives is the imprimatur of our King, signifying that we are followers of the one true God. The human heart is designed by the Creator to respond to the presence of love. Paul refers to this built-in sensitivity when he writes, "The creation eagerly waits for the revealing of the sons of God" (Rom 8:19). Even in its darkened and fallen spiritual state, the world is intuitively looking for the "sons of God."

Once when we were giving out food just before Christmas, we met a woman who confided in us that both she and her husband were unemployed. We gave her food and then offered to pray for her. She received prayer from us although she openly questioned the concept of a benevolent God in light of her recent difficulties.

After we prayed we didn't have any further contact with this woman until almost a year later. Then a few weeks before that next Christmas, she called to tell us that she had finally found a great new job, just what she'd wanted. She was so grateful for what had happened in her life the year before that she wanted to take in donations from the other employees and then give us the money to purchase more food for the needy. Our part in that wonderful answer to prayer was small, but just hearing the results of our little seed was very encouraging.

Proverbs 11:30 promises us that "he who wins souls is wise." You and I will have plenty of job security as we step out to lead others to Christ. There are lots of souls who need winning, each one suffering significant pain in many areas of life. As we touch those pains we will be able to impart a message of hope for a future in Jesus Christ.

One group of students I know offers a tutoring service for struggling underclassmen. It seems only natural to conclude their sessions with a little prayer asking God's help for the upcoming exam. After doing this for over a year now, these godly tutors have received many encouraging stories from students who have seen miracles on their tests. Such positive results provide open doors for further conversations about the God who gives us grace and wisdom in abundance.

CHILDREN ARE NATURALS

"There must be more to life than having everything!"
—**Maurice Sendak**

M OST FAMILIES ARE UNDER increasing time pressures. Statistics show the average American enjoys 17 percent less leisure time now than just ten years ago. In spite of the hectic pace of life, my wife and I make it a priority to take our children out to do service projects twice a month. Janie and I believe that they would be receiving an incomplete spiritual education if they only read Bible stories and spent time in Sunday school. Our children need to learn that getting outside the four walls of the church to interact with the lost and the poor is a normal part of the Christian life.

We take our children along on church buses which have been especially designed for ministry to the poor. We had the seats removed and replaced with racks for food and clothing so that each bus is capable of hauling one hundred fifty bags of groceries and enough clothes to outfit a small army. Once we load up, we drive to various parts of Cincinnati where we can find a concentration of folks in need. Since the poor often lack transportation to reach sources of help, we remedy this by simply going to them! Once we arrive, we turn on some contemporary Christian music and begin to invite the neighborhood out for free food and clothes.

My eight-year-old daughter, Laura, had agreed to go with me on one of these trips, but when Saturday morning rolled around she had become engrossed in watching cartoons. After a little persuasion we reached a compromise: I bribed my daughter by agreeing to take her to McDonald's later if she went. I was amazed how quickly she was dressed and buckled into the waiting car!

After we arrived at an inner city housing project, we began to help people carry bags of groceries from the bus to their apartments. A couple of young mothers got off the bus with their arms overflowing with groceries and clothes. As we walked along chatting with these women, I received a word of knowledge. I "saw" in my mind's eye a picture of a knee with a red light blinking on its left side. I asked the lady if she had a knee problem. She said she did. In the next moment several more specific bits of information came to me. Somehow I knew that she had slipped on a patch of ice in front of her apartment in January. I also knew that her doctor had told her that she would probably need surgery, a prospect which made her fearful.

Laura saw that God uses imperfect people—even her parents! Most of all, she experienced the power of God moving through her very normal, eight-year-old frame.

The woman was flabbergasted as I shared this with her. She said, "I know who you are—a man of God!" She was not just open to our praying for her, she was enthusiastic! I had Laura place *her hand* on the woman's knee and coached her in praying for the power of God to remove the pain and damaged tissue. To Laura's amazement, she saw the presence of the Lord come upon her. The damaged knee became warm and the part that had been hurting felt numb to the woman.

I was excited about God's work of healing, but wanted to share this as more of a *perspective* story than a *power* story. Laura experienced something very powerful that morning that might easily stick with her the rest of her life. She saw God touch a woman in a dynamic way. She saw that God uses imperfect people—even her parents! Most of all, she experienced the power of God moving through her very normal, eight-year-old frame.

The church of today needs a new perspective on the role of children in ministering to the needs of others. They are capable of being used powerfully. The boy Samuel proved that he could hear God's call, accurately discern God's will, and even prophesy regarding the future. Too often children have been seen only as the *future* church, when in reality they are a vital part of the church today, whatever their age. Unless we can give these little ones a more important role in outreach we will miss the opportunity of having some of our best evangelists touch the world. For their own sake, our children need to grow up in a home built not on a theory of Christianity but on the ongoing expression of God's love and grace to others.

CHILDREN—OUR BEST EVANGELISTS

On Palm Sunday, Jesus admonished the Jewish leaders that if the people were quiet the very rocks would cry out in praise (Lk 19:29-40). I have sometimes wondered why the Lord *didn't* use rocks. They are plentiful, obedient, and always ready. People, on the other hand, are fickle and undependable. Young children are a lot like rocks. They are plentiful, usually obedient, and consistently more available than adults. Unlike adults, children don't set so many conditions on their obedience. It's possible that children are the church's best evangelists. Consider that possibility with me.

Children are available. One of the most powerful miracles in the Gospels comes through the obedience, purity, and innocence of a little boy. After Jesus had been teaching for a couple of days, the crowd of several thousand people had grown hungry. Since the town was too distant, the apostles went through the crowd asking, "Who has food they can share?"

The bad news for the apostles was that only a small bit of food was available—just the lunch of a young boy. I believe others probably had food, but none of the adults were willing to share. They rationalized their way out of offering their own meager sustenance. For practical purposes, the only food available was the lunch prepared by the boy's mother, some loaves and fish.

Jesus didn't seem concerned. After giving thanks for what God had made available, he directed the apostles to distribute food to those gathered on the hillside. I believe that little lunch didn't suddenly turn into a gigantic mound of bread and fish, but kept appearing bit by bit as the disciples began to hand it out. Jesus makes it clear that a little, combined with the presence of God, adds up to plenty for even a crowd of thousands to eat more than their fill.

During the busy summer season many people find it difficult to maintain their lawns, so we load several lawn mowers into trucks and drive about the neighborhoods of Cincinnati looking for long grass. It's really easy for our lawn crews to spot who needs ministry. As we drove up to one house, we could hear the sound of the Reds baseball game filtering through the screen door. Our team leader knocked on the door and explained what we wanted to do. A man sat emotionless in an Archie-Bunker style easy chair—in front of the tube with beer in hand. His only response was, "Sure, go ahead and cut my grass. Whatever." We were surprised he didn't react to our unusual offer. How often does someone stop by and offer to cut your grass for free?

The team made quick work of the unkempt lawn. Within thirty minutes we had cut, edged, and bagged all the grass. The leader knocked at the door to tell the man that we had done this to show him God's love in a way he could understand. His response was again fairly unemotional, "OK. Thanks."

As they walked down the porch steps, ten-year-old Adam told his dad the Lord had given him a word of knowledge. We have trained the children of our church to see it as natural to receive such words from the Lord when he wants to touch someone. We have also incorporated praying for the sick into our regular Sunday school curriculum. Adam's words of knowledge had proven to be accurate on several other occasions, so the adults on this particular outing took him seriously.

Adam sensed that the Lord wanted us to pray for this man that his pain be relieved. We didn't know what his pain was, but we cautiously went forward to take advantage of this apparent opportunity. After mowing the lawn the team felt they had enough of a connection to step out in boldness and say, "Before leaving we want to just pray for you briefly."

The man reluctantly agreed. Since Adam had gotten the word it was only appropriate that he should pray. As they stood in a circle, the boy offered a prayer that was simple and to the point: "Lord, come now and relieve the pain in this man's heart."

What followed next amazed even these veteran servant evangelists. The man began to sob uncontrollably! After a few minutes he had thoroughly wet the shoulder of the person nearest him. After his emotions calmed down, the man explained that his wife had been hospitalized for surgery. His nineteen-year-old son had been caught just the previous night stealing a car to support his drug habit. This man had been sitting in his living room that morning feeling absolutely overwhelmed by these family troubles.

This story highlights some of the advantages children have over more sophisticated adult believers. The grown-up team members placed a premium on time and were ready to go on to the next house. Because this child wasn't in any hurry at all, he was able to realize that the purposes of God were not yet fulfilled. Adults tend to be fearful of looking bad in public, so they were slow to suggest praying for a stranger. Without Adam's simple prayer perhaps this man's heart would not have been unlocked to receive God's comfort.

◆◆◆

Adam has no problem believing that God is real,
and *that God wants to use him to*
influence the world.

◆◆◆

Just as important was what happened to Adam himself. I have spoken to his parents several times about that day. They believe that something significant was planted in Adam's heart when he saw the man radically touched as a fruit of his prayer. While children learn by what they are told, they are always more likely to remember what they experience. This young boy has no problem believing that God is real, *and* that God wants to use him to influence the world. Many adult believers don't really believe that God wants to use them or even could use them if they made themselves available.

Children have credibility. Several years ago, I saw something regarding children in ministry that was odd yet enlightening. One of the course requirements for a Bible college class on the cults was to attend a meeting of the Jehovah's Witnesses at the local Kingdom Hall. Having never been to a meeting of a cultic group, I found the evening intimidating and was glad that a couple of friends came along as moral support.

The meeting consisted mainly of leaders doing a little bit of Bible teaching and mostly exhorting the people to get out and evangelize more. At several points in the evening they practiced their witnessing skills by role-playing with others in the group. One aspect of their meetings I found very interesting was their use of children to do evangelism. Though their belief system is riddled with unbiblical perceptions of God and life, I had to admire their insight for letting children open doors to people's hearts. These young Jehovah's Witnesses resembled little robots, spouting off memorized party lines of church doctrines. The leaders knew that while most people wouldn't hesitate to slam the door on an adult door-knocker, the public is probably not going to be rude to a child.

Children are disarming. While we never want to *use* children, they do cause outsiders to take notice of God. Inside every adult, just beneath the skin, is a child who has some idea of God. Children serve as a reminder of the simplicity of our relationship with God. When they tell someone, "We're serving you to show you God's love," adults listen.

I never like to see children spouting off spiritual truth which is not real to them. In fact, they don't need to say much. Children effectively model God's love simply by being children. By their simplicity and trust, they depict the clearest picture of a lifestyle which is obedient to the Lord Jesus. Perhaps it was for these qualities that Jesus said we must become as little children to enter the kingdom of God (Mt 18:3).

Children are the doorway into the church for outsiders. When children speak (or cry), it seems people really listen. My wife Janie and I noticed this when our first child was just a few months old. We were amazed to see that just about everybody loves babies. We would go into restaurants and complete strangers would smile and begin to talk to us about their children or grandchildren. Before long we would naturally get into other topics, often talking about God. It seems that the presence of children inclines our thoughts toward God. For example, when children come along in their marriage, many baby boomers who may have avoided organized religion seek out a church home.

I recently met a woman in her mid-seventies at a newcomers' coffee. I naturally asked how she happened to come to our church. She told me a heartwarming story. This woman was housebound for several months after her back was broken in an accident. One Sunday morning, she was lying on the couch watching a TV preacher and wishing she were well enough to go to church. Just then her doorbell rang. Standing on her porch were a couple of boys with an adult supervisor and a marigold plant.

These two boys were part of a class which trains children in areas such as ministry to the poor, praying for the sick, and being members of "God's Secret Service" (servant evangelism boiled down to a child's level). We offer these classes during the summers as an alternative to our normal Sunday school program. Our goal is to provide opportunities where they can actually *see* the working of God.

When this woman opened her door they explained, "We're giving out plants this morning to show God's love to you in a practical way." She was so touched by the gesture that she cried even in retelling the story months afterward. When she got better she decided to find out what kind of Christians would give away flowers to show God's love. She came and decided to join.

Children are fearless! Researchers report that all of us are born with just a handful of natural fears which are oriented to self-preservation. Out of those basic survival instincts, less healthy fears crop up. As we get older, living in fear becomes for many of us a way of life. Unless we learn how to deal with our fears, we often become even more cautious as we grow older.

Most adults are reticent to do any sort of outreach because they fear failure. We've been conditioned to think that failure is a painful thing that ought to be avoided. The truth is that failure is the necessary doorway to growing and learning about most things in life. Children haven't been conditioned to play it safe. Most of them are free from the fears that plague and even paralyze adults.

For example, how many adults do you know who would be willing to sell candy at the neighborhood grocery store? It seems that every time I go shopping at the local supermarket I see children from soccer leagues or Little League or Girl Scouts selling candy by the exit. I'm a sucker for kids selling things so I always buy something even though I don't like candy!

One church I know of in the New York City area doesn't allow fear of danger to hinder their evangelistic efforts. With adult oversight a small army of children goes out into the neighborhood in a variety of creative ways. They regularly touch four to five hundred people within a couple of hours through free face painting, helium balloons, Polaroid photos, and cold drinks. In that setting it is only natural for these young evangelists to tell the neighborhood children about Christ. The parents have been so impressed by such friendliness that many new families have been added to the church.

BENEFITS TO CHILDREN WHEN THEY DO SERVANT EVANGELISM

Some enormous benefits come to the children whose families regularly reach out to serve their communities through these kinds of projects. Let's consider a few of these growth points.

Children become outward in an age of introversion. The electronic age has shaped our lives toward inwardness. By adolescence the average child has become well acquainted with cable TV, take-out food, video games, phones, computers, mail-order sales, telephones, faxes, portable stereos with headphones, and VCRs. Although these conveniences can serve a useful purpose, they also encourage us to spend a significant amount of time by ourselves. Many of us spend too much time alone, creating an ever-shrinking circle of relationships.

In her book *The Popcorn Report,* futurist Faith Popcorn calls this increasing trend in America "cocooning," digging into our "high-tech caves" as a way to remain safe from the intimidating world about us. Popcorn projects that it will soon be possible to hole up for weeks, maybe even months, at a time without leaving the security of our homes.[1]

The Christian community is no stranger to this phenomenon of cocooning. I spoke recently with a man who attended Christian schools from nursery school through graduate school. At the end of nearly two decades of being sheltered, he discovered that he had been poorly prepared for life in the real world. After coming out of his spiritual funk, this man confided in me that he wanted to develop a new, realistic Christian life that included those who don't yet know Jesus Christ. Servant evangelism provides a practical way to encourage this outward directedness at a younger age.

Children become sensitive to the moving of the Holy Spirit. Youngsters seem to feel at home with the idea that God can work through them, but this natural sensitivity is soon lost if it remains untapped. The best way for children to grow in their awareness of the Holy Spirit's action is through firsthand experience. The presence of the Lord is not an idea to be mastered in the context of a book, but a heart knowledge which becomes real as we minister to others. Serving large numbers of people convinces our children (and us) that something unique is happening with each person we touch.

The presence of the Lord is not an idea to be
mastered in the context of a book,
but a heart knowledge which becomes real
as we minister to others.

Something wells up in people as they see the Spirit moving in clear ways upon others. Jesus tells us that "the eye is the lamp of the body" (Mt 6:22, RSV). What we see through our "lamps" is taken into our hearts. When children see people being healed and empowered through the gifts of the Holy Spirit, they themselves become hungry to be touched and used by God. When children see God move, I believe that something is planted *inside* of them which will last a lifetime.

As children see their parents minister, they will know that the life of God is real. One of the most popular television shows in recent years is *The Simpsons,* a sitcom which pokes fun at parent-child relationships. Like any caricature, the humor merely exaggerates the reality of typical family life. Children certainly have plenty of opportunities to see the weaknesses and shortcomings of their parents. As parents we need to continually find new ways of showing the life of the Lord to our children.

Scripture promises us that if we "train up a child in the way he should go,... when he is old he will not depart from it" (Prv 22:6). That training goes far beyond imparting information. We must show them Jesus, the Son of God who is the way, the truth, and the life. Children learn and grow by doing, not just by hearing Bible stories and doing "sword" drills. Authentic change happens from the inside out. We need to model for our children how the life of God changes us as agents of his grace going out into our communities.

It is vital that children see their parents express their beliefs in clear ways, both by word and deed. Experts tell us that only about 10 percent of our communication is done verbally. We constantly model our attitudes through our behavior. Our children will pay a lot more attention to what we do than to what we say. Children must see that following Jesus Christ involves *obeying* the will of God as well as *learning* the will of God. They need to have parents who not only *know* the truth but also live the truth of God.

As parents we must regularly ask ourselves, "What sort of Christianity am I living out before my children? Do I reflect a healthy balance between receiving and giving the life of God, or do I resemble the Dead Sea that takes in much but gives off little and grows saltier year by year?" The brand of Christianity our children adopt will probably look a lot like that which we have demonstrated, despite the correct Christian words we may have spoken along the way.

HOW TO TAKE YOUR FAMILY
INTO THE COMMUNITY

We are living in an age of unbelievable rebellion and confusion, a time when children can even go to court and divorce their parents. Increasingly negative news edges out the few positive reports on the horizon. As society becomes more and more dangerous, especially for children, our natural response is to run away and hide. The church serves many believers as primarily a secure shelter *from* the world. A more biblical response is to run wisely into the world.

We are called to let the light of Christ pierce the surrounding darkness. Invading this darkness isn't as impossible as it may seem. Here are some tips I've discovered in bringing light into the darkness with my family.

Start with a simple, *"safe"* project. A primary goal in taking your children out to do service projects is to provide positive experiences with evangelism. We want to build up their courage which can overflow into more advanced areas of ministry later on. All of the servant evangelism projects listed in appendix one are generally nonthreatening. Go with the ones that appeal to you.

One consideration is the age and abilities of your children. For example, it would probably not be a good idea to take small children out washing windshields because they aren't tall enough to reach. Even older children are likely to streak the windows because they often don't have a well developed eye for detail. Another case of project incompatibility with children occurs every time we conduct a car wash. Without fail a small child will want to hold one of the hoses. That is not a good idea. Most kids lack enough skill or good judgment when it comes to controlling a running hose. When everyone gets wet, including the people we're trying to serve, we end up leaving a poor impression.

A more manageable car wash alternatative would be to have children wash the wheels or the bumpers. Another easy and sure-fire project involves distributing drinks in front of a grocery store on a Saturday morning. Plugging parking meters is also a favorite for children who are tall enough. Meanwhile an adult could slip a little flyer under the windshield wiper.

For the past several summers several dozen churches around the country have sponsored a program called Summer of Service or S.O.S. We take young people from high school or college who are considering the ministry as a profession and try to give them a safe and positive experience with different sorts of outreach. Many of these students are petrified at the thought of going out to the community with God's love. After just a few days of serving, a significant breakthrough frequently occurs. Once they've gotten a positive evangelism experience under their belt, they more easily assume greater degrees of risk in ministry.

Be *wise*—supervise! Without question we live in dangerous times, but children can learn valuable lessons for life by getting out into the real world under proper supervision. It is imperative that we proceed with wisdom when doing service projects. Before we even go out, we discuss with the children some of the realities of the world in which we live. We are coming with the mercy and compassion of God, but because of the state of the world, some of those we serve are hurting and even seriously disturbed. Some safety guidelines we follow on ministry outings with children include the following:

All ministry is conducted with adults: As adults we do almost all of our ministry in teams. This principle is especially important for children. Some places we visit are unsavory. We don't necessarily need to avoid going to those places, we just go at certain times of the day when we feel safe. And we always go with plenty of adult supervision.

Children must always stay with adult supervisors: Children can talk to strangers, but only in the presence of adult leaders. We always tell the children that they are never to leave the area where the service project is taking place. In providing a positive experience, we allow the children to do most of the ministry, with the adults looking over their shoulder. Depending on the project and the age of the children, we keep things manageable by having at least one adult for every three children.

Go out with your children *regularly.* I recommend that you plan several ministry outings in advance or else you'll find yourself going out only once in a great while. Ideally, I'd shoot for going out once per month. Saturday morning works well for many families. I recommend that you not attempt projects that require longer than two hours. The goal here is to quit before it feels like drudgery to your children. It's better to leave them having fun instead of driving the project into the ground. With younger children who have even shorter attention spans, you will need to plan accordingly.

The goal is to quit before it feels like drudgery to your children. It's better to leave them having fun instead of driving the project into the ground.

After going out, spend time *downloading.* Go out after your project for a burger and a time of sharing. This is an ideal time to get feedback from the child's perspective. While it's still fresh in their minds, ask them to share any victories, insights, or fears they felt while serving. Children need help interpreting their ministry experiences. Remember, you are building lasting memories which will help to mold their views about God, life, and your own Christianity.

Seek to make ministry *fun!* Over the years we have coined an expression that is *almost* straight from Scripture: "Where the

Spirit of the Lord is, there is fun!" More than anything else, the best guarantee for influencing your children with the kingdom of God is to make your ministry time fun! The only activities any of us do long-term are those we enjoy. Children are especially motivated to seek fun. With ministry I've seen that if I'm not having fun, neither will my children.

If children observe their parents serving out of duty or sheer commitment, they will get a bad taste in their mouths for church, ministry, and perhaps even for God. I am convinced that duty-oriented Christianity has turned many more children off to the Lord than any recognized enemy of the faith such as secular humanism. If you present an attractive and enjoyable picture of what it means to be a Christian, they are more likely to see it as something they can commit themselves to for life. And most importantly, they will build a picture of a God that is positive and approachable.

One tool we use is to hold a monthly "Matthew's Party." This is a takeoff on the party recorded in Luke 5 where Matthew throws a celebration to mark his conversion to following Jesus as the Messiah. In his joy, Matthew invited his friends who had never met Jesus to have dinner with the Lord. We also sponsor a party in a particular neighborhood and invite everyone to have dinner with the Lord and us.

For a video of Matthew's Party write or call:
Vineyard Community Church
11340 Century Circle East
Cincinnati, Ohio 45246
Phone: 513-671-0422
www.kindness.com

At one Matthew's Party we drew over one thousand guests from an inner city neighborhood. We hung our twenty-foot wide banner that reads, "It's Party Time!" We fired up our grill on wheels that can roast three hundred hot dogs at a time. We put on loud music and called the neighborhood out to have fun with us. Basically we took over the better part of the park adjoining a low-income housing project. Entire families from our church attended because this outreach involved some sort of ministry for every adult and child.

As I looked around it was heartwarming to see so much practical love being shared with a hurting neighborhood. One group was fixing and cleaning a swing set. Another cluster of folks was clipping weeds and sweeping up broken glass. Others were leading organized games for the neighborhood children. About twenty adults and children dressed up as clowns and did silly stuff. Still another group was tossing frisbees around the park with kids from the housing projects. Positive bonds were being formed everywhere around the party.

◆◆◆

"Thanks for putting this on. There is something almost tangible of the Lord's presence here. You can almost feel him here in the park. I know this is making a powerful impact on my son. Today he has seen and felt what I've been telling him about God all his life."

◆◆◆

One of the parents from our church came up to me in the midst of all this activity and said, "Thanks for putting this on. There is something almost tangible of the Lord's presence here. You can almost feel him here in the park. I know this is making a powerful impact on my son. Today he has seen and felt what I've been telling him about God all his life."

Jesus wants all of us to head toward matching our works with our words. To do so we're going to need new leaders who are free from the fears that have held back so many believers. What more appropriate group from whom to learn boldness than our children.

SMALL GROUPS TURNED INSIDE OUT

"It is one of the most beautiful compensations of life that no man can sincerely try to help another without helping himself."
—Ralph Waldo Emerson

W HEN MY CHURCH WAS STILL SMALL, we started meeting together in support groups made up of five or so members. My group consisted of a machinist, a female karate instructor (a black belt), a receptionist, a sales agent, and a homemaker. We had little in common outside of our relationship with Jesus Christ, but that glue was strong enough to bind us together in love.

Most churches include several groups that meet for a variety of purposes. These smaller clusters offer support on a more personal level as well as an opportunity to develop deeper relationships. Most groups, if left to themselves, will grow cozy and closed. Newcomers are often tolerated rather than heartily welcomed and find it difficult to break in. One of the best ways to avoid ingrown groups is to have them practice servant evangelism together.

On the second night in a new group, we began discussing a plan for outreach. One spontaneous person said, "Why don't we go out right now! We'll pack some bags of food and be on our way." I myself am typically more calculated in my approach to ministry, but a group-think dynamic seized everyone and before I could add a word of caution we were on our way! We decided to give away food in a nearby housing area where many needy families lived. We went to the store, bought some generic food, and packed our bags into a station wagon. Then our group split into twos and decided to reconvene an hour later.

A group-think dynamic seized everyone and before I could add a word of caution we were on our way!

Our approach was simple: we would knock on doors, offer food, and ask if we could pray for any needs. My partner and I gave away four bags of food to several families. Twice we met families who said, "We could use some food, but so-and-so is *really* in need of food. Why don't you give it to them and if you have any left over come back here." Another single mom we met said she not only needed food but was wondering what it meant to be a Christian. After a short explanation of the gospel, we were able to pray with her to invite Jesus Christ into her heart.

The hour of designated time seemed to fly by, as if we had entered some kind of time warp. We gathered back together to share stories of our personal encounters. Some of them seemed almost unbelievable. One other team had prayed with someone to accept Jesus as Savior. Another had run into a family that had been out of food for a couple of days and weren't scheduled to receive food stamps for another week.

Still another pair had met a woman whose arm was paralyzed from a recent stroke. They had prayed a simple prayer, "Come Lord and heal this woman's arm." If they hadn't brought her with them, I wouldn't have believed the amazing results. In front of me stood a grandmotherly woman who enthusiastically reported to me that she had felt an instant, mild, electrical shock flow through her shoulder and arm to her fingertips. Feeling in her arm and even mobility in her fingers returned.

We were all stunned. What we saw is the stuff the Book of Acts is written about. Several years later, that evening still stands out as one of the most spectacular of my life. We saw for the first time that God works in wonderful ways through common believers who step out to do the ministry of Jesus in our neighborhoods. I had prayed for the sick before and I had given out plenty of bags of groceries. Frankly, something good happened in most of my attempts at outreach, but most of the time I had operated as a "Lone Ranger."

I realized through this experience that God *really* likes to move through a group that steps out to serve the needs of others. Groups have proven to be the greenhouse which allows the life of the Holy Spirit to flourish in our midst. At this point our church has grown to include over two hundred small groups—ranging from those focused on fellowship to Bible studies, women's groups, men's groups, recovery groups, or "affinity" groups who gather around a common interest such as bicycling, fishing, or a creative craft of some sort.

Your church probably has many groups already in place—such as a choir, a women's circle, or various boards and committees— each of which has a distinct identity and focus. Each group could be a closed circle that exists to itself alone, or it could be a bridge which takes the life of God out into the community. Try an experiment: cut your meeting time in half and go out to wash windshields. I predict that your group will develop a new level of intimacy as a result of this shared task. As groups cultivate a value for reaching out beyond themselves, they are much more likely to survive and to create an atmosphere of healing for its members.

A LIGHTHOUSE SHINES OUTWARD

I have been in some small group continuously for almost thirty years now. The idea of going out to serve in the community has always seemed foreign at first, but I have discovered that groups who don't reach outside of themselves don't last long. They typically turn inward and become consumed with the stress of their own interpersonal problems. Relational conflict will eventually erode a group from the inside out.

Each group is a potential lighthouse with the combined brilliance of each member's spiritual flashlight pointed into the spiritually darkened community. The powerful light of the Spirit of God in us has the capacity to shine far beyond itself. Groups which are not focusing outwardly can easily end up shining those flashlights into the eyes of one another. That can easily prove to be distracting if not dangerous.

The local church, whatever its size, doesn't seem to make sense unless it is giving itself away to the world around it. I know of a group that began reaching out to the homeless in a neighborhood park. They prepared meals for several dozen people and offered coffee and conversation afterward. Their willingness to step out and serve was gradually rewarded with increased momentum. After two years old they were still reaching out regularly to the homeless, with an annual budget of $35,000 which they raise through tithing and donations.

The church begins to function as the church when we reach out into the community. I can think of several reasons why we ought to reach out.

Jesus launched the church through a small group. The church of Jesus Christ looked fairly unimpressive in the first chapter of Acts. After three years of training and modeling, Jesus was taken up before his disciples to return to the Father. They must have stood on the Mount of Olives staring up in both awe and shock: awe because they were in the presence of the glory of God, but also stunned and amazed at the final words of Jesus when he offered his strategy for winning the world: "You will be witnesses to me" (Acts 1:8).

At that moment this small group of disciples felt far from being empowered witnesses for Christ. They must have felt more like fearful failures. Things hadn't been going so well recently. One of their friends had betrayed Jesus and eventually committed suicide. The authorities were making threats and possibly coming after them. And now, wouldn't you know it, Jesus had departed for good! I think they were so shocked that they didn't know what to do next. Finally a couple of angels appeared and reiterated the words of Jesus: they were to return to Jerusalem and wait for the Lord's empowering.

This was just a small group, not so very different from some groups you and I have been a part of. For three years they watched Jesus bend the laws of nature with his miracles, speak the very words of God to the masses, and even raise the dead. For the past forty days they had witnessed the resurrected Jesus walk through walls and witness to the Spirit's power to bring the dead back to life through faith in God. Things seemed to be moving toward a crescendo.

*"He couldn't have said we would be his witnesses.
Why, just look at us! We're shaking like leaves.
We can't give his kingdom away. That would
never work. Angels would be much better at this
than us. They don't get scared and they're so much
more mobile, being able to fly and all."*

At last, on the hillside outside Jerusalem, Jesus gives his secret for touching the world with the power of God: "You eleven will be my witnesses." They must have thought they heard wrong. I can just imagine the disciples saying something like, "He couldn't have said we would be his witnesses. Why, just look at us! We're shaking like leaves. We can't give his kingdom away. That would never work. Angels would be much better at this than us. They don't get scared and they're so much more mobile, being able to fly and all."

They shouldn't have been all that surprised. Jesus had already made it apparent that he really likes to minister in small groups. The apostles had been part of a small group for the past three years. With the exception of a few miracles, all of Jesus' works had been done in the presence of his small group, the apostles. Jesus had encouraged them to travel about ministering in groups as well because the life of the Holy Spirit is energized when two or three are gathered in his name (Mt 18:20). If the world would be won, the life of God would go forward through small bands of people truly loving one another and sharing that love with others.

Shared outreach experiences knit a group together. When groups focus beyond themselves, lives are changed and bettered, from the first person we pray for, feed, or serve. "Remember when" stories provide a solid core of growth. A deep spiritual power permeates a group when they share a mission beyond themselves. The incarnational life of God flows through them to create an environment that builds a sense of family. When someone sees God move through him or her and that moment occurs in the presence of others, a special bonding takes place. That experience is frozen in time as a unique moment in spiritual history. Your group will never be the same after they have gone out into the community to minister together.

Outreach raises the level of spiritual health in each group member's life. From the beginning all of our groups have had one or more special people we affectionately call EGRs—"Extra Grace Required." This helpful term coined by Dale Galloway describes individuals who have lots of special needs. Most of the time this sort of person has more issues than a group can take on successfully. All EGRs will show some improvement when attention is shown them and they do tend to get better, gradually and slowly.

If unchecked and not given boundaries, an energetic EGR can actually kill a healthy group. I've seen it happen occasionally. As a hurting person enters a group and gives off distress signals, the group takes that person on as an assignment. If they are not careful, however, the purpose of the group can become getting that person healed. Most EGRs are probably never going to be fully healed in the context of the group. They've been peculiar for a long time and they may be that way the rest of their lives.

We need to signal to needy group members that we expect them to get better by giving themselves away along with the rest of us. Perhaps they aren't capable of doing sophisticated outreach that requires much emotional energy, but just about anyone can wash a windshield. I invited one older woman out with us who had been through some very traumatic episodes recently. I told her that she would probably see an increase in the grace of God in her life as she gave herself away to others in greater need than herself. Since she couldn't physically manage washing windshields, I put her in charge of passing out the squeegees and refilling the bottles of cleaning liquid. At the end of the day she agreed that the life of God had touched her as she reached out with the good news.

An action orientation helps to identify budding leaders. What is a leader? A simple functional definition is "someone who leads others." In our day the word brings to mind the person with the most information or the one with the longest time spent as a Christian. In some groups it would be the one who has graduated from a respected school. All these marks are good and even part of the picture, but in the end it's the one who leads who is truly a leader.

Nature versus nurture has long been debated in church circles. One group says, "We can produce a leader out of anyone provided they're given adequate oversight." The other group would disagree by saying, "Leaders are born, not made." My experience causes me to fall between these two opinions. I don't think just anyone can be shaped into a leader without some natural gifting.

On the other hand, no one will lead effectively without help from mature and godly believers.

Arguments aside, that mysterious quality called leadership becomes clear when group momentum picks up steam. When activity commences, those who must lead come forth. If a fire were to erupt in a movie theater, the leader would be the one who knew the way out of the building. A leader is simply the person who knows the next step the group needs to take.

The person who is excited about what's going on, who comes early and stays late, who gives sacrificially, who is available—those are the identifiable marks of someone being raised up by the Lord as a leader in servant evangelism.

We can offer potential leaders a test to measure their personality type and background to see if they fit the general picture of a leader, or we can take a more practical approach. Groups that focus on giving themselves away will spontaneously produce leaders. It becomes obvious who is leading in a group which is doing ministry. The person who is excited about what's going on, who comes early and stays late, who gives sacrificially, who is available—those are the identifiable marks of someone being raised up by the Lord as a leader in servant evangelism.

Most people are too shy to do outreach by themselves. The concept of sharing the good news of Jesus Christ usually prompts thoughts of "personal evangelism." The common scenario involves one lone individual sharing Christ with an unbeliever. I often ask the participants of my seminars on evangelism what percentage of them regularly engage in some form of evangelism. Such an impromptu survey consistently reveals that less than 25 percent are regularly sharing Christ, and of those, a very small number have actually experienced praying with someone to ask Christ into their lives.

In short, the evangelical church in America is not very evangelical. We could hazard a pretty safe bet that effective and widespread outreach will not happen with individual Christians going out into the community. It is just too scary for most people to step out in this way. We've all heard that there is safety in numbers. I've discovered more importantly that there is courage to do evangelism in numbers.

For the past couple of years I have helped train small group leaders of a multi-ethnic church on the East Coast. The total membership of about one thousand is made up of some twenty-five different ethnic and language groups. Clustering them according to their native languages seemed to make the foreign city less foreboding.

The Filipino groups had a great desire to win their fellow compatriots to Christ, but found it difficult to make connections because of the hustle and bustle of the city. Conventional personal evangelism seemed too forward and unnatural for their cultural values. Because high blood pressure is a common genetic problem that runs in their families, these groups came up with the idea of doing blood pressure checks in the entryways of large apartment buildings frequented by other Filipinos. Now these groups are meeting dozens of their fellow citizens with each outreach and are able to invite them into their group's social events.

Doors of opportunity will open for a group that won't open for an individual. As we use groups to reach out into our communities we can affect neighbors we'd never be able to get in touch with on our own. A small group leader in our church had been trying to figure out a way to evangelize his upper-middle-class neighborhood on Cincinnati's north side for several years. He rejected conventional methods as offensive to that population, most of whom are overworked and tired. After living in the same house for three years, this man still didn't know most of the neighbors around him and they didn't seem interested in talking to him.

One evening, instead of their regular meeting format, everyone in his group was issued a dozen light bulbs and sent into the neighborhood. As they went from house to house the members identified themselves as part of the group that met at this man's house and offered each homeowner a free light bulb just to show God's love in a practical way. The people in the neighborhood opened up immediately! Lots of positive comments were reported later on, but most importantly, this man is now known throughout his neighborhood as the "light-bulb guy." Now people stop to thank him. They also know that this guy is a Christian, that a group meets at his house, and that these people put their money where their mouth is.

Our impact is greater than the sum of our actual numbers when we work in groups. Servant evangelism projects draw attention because of their novelty, but a team also presents the appearance of being all over the place. When our budding church had just a few dozen members, four to eight of them would typically show up whenever we sponsored an outreach project. One Saturday morning we had three people doing a free windshield wash at one location. A block away we had another group of three going door to door raking leaves. As I washed their windshields, several people asked, "Are you with those people down the street who are raking leaves? How big is your church anyway? You people are *everywhere*." We were actually just a handful.

"Are you with those people down the street who are raking leaves? How big is your church anyway? You people are everywhere."

More recently, a group of about twenty participated in four different projects at a shopping area near downtown. We managed to intersect over one thousand people during our ninety minute outreach and truly gave the impression of being a massive army. When Christians decide to reach out we become like the tiny mustard seed that grows and spreads into the community beyond all proportion. Even with small numbers we can get the attention of the world around us.

The life of Christ shines brightly through a group. Serving in a group creates an *atmosphere* of evangelism with joy as the primary by-product. The Spirit of Christ, the ultimate servant, fills us and surrounds us in a way which is very appealing to outsiders. Paul describes that presence as the "fragrance of Christ among those who are being saved and among those who are perishing" (2 Cor 2:15). Though they probably can't give words to its reality, our goal is to create a tangible experience of God's love as people encounter the life of Christ in us.

I recently heard about a young man who became convinced of the reality of God's life through encountering a small group. A Christian friend had patiently explained the good news of Christ to this fellow on several occasions, but he seemed unresponsive. On his way out the door to do some shopping, this nonbeliever finally exclaimed to his Christian buddy, "Look, I'm not going to listen to anymore of what you have to say until you so-called Christians begin to show this love you're telling me about. I've heard about all the talk I can take."

Literally, at that very moment, they heard a knock at the door. They opened it to find part of a small group giving away light bulbs as a servant evangelism project. When he was greeted with, "Hi, I'd like to give you a light bulb to show you God's love in a practical way," the young man was stunned. Guess what was at the top of his shopping list? Light bulbs. He got what he insisted was necessary before he'd believe—*experiencing* the love of God through Christians. A few days later this man came to Christ and is now attending the same church as the small group.

One small group of about ten has been going to a popular bicycle path every other Sunday afternoon to serve Gatorade to bikers and walkers. For the few minutes they stand there and drink, each passerby is in the presence of the Lord through his people. Even through a brief conversation, they can watch the believers in action and see how they relate to the public and one another. On a recent "Gatorade outing" some group members left the area for a few minutes. When they returned they clearly noticed something around the outreach area. Even a few feet away felt entirely different, but up close to the Gatorade jug they felt a clear sense of the presence of the Lord. When several of our lights are shining at once, they take on added brilliance.

How Can Small Groups Begin Doing Kindness Evangelism?

Small groups function more effectively according to certain guidelines. Here are a few practical thoughts from our own experience on how to launch groups into the community.

Discover what projects will work for your group. It is important that a group feel ownership of this approach in general and any particular projects you decide to undertake. Discuss the philosophy behind servant evangelism and brainstorm as to what might work in your neck of the woods. Because people's needs tend to be quite different from place to place, what flies in one part of town might go over like a lead balloon just a few blocks away. Ask God for wisdom.

Your small group may already have its finger on the pulse of the community more clearly than your church leaders, who tend to focus more on meeting the needs of the members. Ask yourselves as a group what needs are present in your circles of influence. Begin to address those which are immediately clear. Once you've seized those opportunities, more clarity will come to you. Before long you'll be tapped into the unique projects that fit your community.

Don't apply pressure to the leadership of the local church to take charge of launching into servant evangelism. Most pastors welcome evangelistic efforts but simply don't have the time or emotional stamina to lead something else personally. Depending on the local church government, obtain the minimal amount of permission required by explaining to the pertinent leaders what you have in mind. Then step out and begin to serve. Your success is the fastest way to spread this outreach among other groups. As good stories begin to circulate, you'll get the attention and affirmation of the church leaders.

Go out once every four to six weeks. Each group needs to decide how often they can go out to do ministry projects without overextending themselves. Our groups don't necessarily meet every week; some meet twice or even once per month depending on the schedules and needs of the members. I recommend that you go out once every fourth or fifth time you meet. If you meet just twice a month, that means you'd go out about every other month for a project. If your group meets every week, you'd go out about once a month. Because of the hurried pace of life most of us face, you'll probably find it necessary to exchange one of your normal meeting times for an outreach project. We all have lots of "good things" happening in our lives. It's difficult to get excited about another event being added on top of an already stressed-out schedule.

If you are a leader, give your group permission to minister. Leaders of small groups need to *regularly* give people permission to go out into the community to do ministry. They also need to keep explaining that such involvement is perfectly fine for laypeople. Most Christians have to unlearn the centuries-old mentality of waiting for the clergy or trained professionals to lead the way. Martin Luther wanted to see each believer view himself or herself as a priest or minister, but sadly that aspect of the Reformation has never taken hold. Few pastors would object to having their people doing ministry in the community.

Value spontaneity. It isn't all that complicated to show deeds of kindness. Sometimes I find it refreshing to surprise everyone in the group by dropping the normal weekly plan and going out to serve. (Not all groups I've been in like being surprised, so use wisdom here.) Some of our most positive experiences have risen out of observing a need and then reasoning, "Hey, we could do something about that need. Let's go help!"

A woman in one of our groups noticed that many women shoppers at a local, self-serve grocery were trying to simultaneously pack their grocery bags, tend to their children, and write a check. Most of them happily saved money on groceries at this store, but getting out the door was difficult. The group leader went to the store manager and offered to have some of his people pack bags at the checkout stand, while others escorted the shoppers to their cars and helped unload the groceries. These simple services were greatly appreciated.

Don't tire people with long projects. One important practical note: when you go out as a group it's wise to usually keep your outings to a maximum of two hours. The idea here is to go out long enough to do some significant serving, but to finish your projects before it becomes work. For many of us that crossover point occurs at two hours. Much beyond two hours also becomes more difficult for most people to schedule into their lives on any regular basis.

I recommend that you begin any two-hour project with a brief time of instruction and conclude with a possible time of debriefing at the end, bringing your total time to about two and a half hours. We usually gather at 9:45 on Saturday mornings, are gone by ten o'clock, and then gather back at a given location at noon to share stories of how things went.

Consider funding your own projects within the group. If your church doesn't have enough money to fund your projects, take up a little offering among yourselves for equipment and supplies. Most of the ideas contained in appendix one are simple and low in cost. If you need equipment, I recommend that you not put an expectation upon the church as a whole to finance your outreach. This idea is rather unusual. It may easily take some time to convince the leaders that servant evangelism succeeds at touching people with God's love. A small investment in simple equipment will enable you to launch out. When the fruit becomes more apparent, perhaps local church financing will become available.

Don't worry about mistakes. Remember that God blesses action and obedience, even if you make mistakes! He loves to provide guidance, but we must take the first step. If you are a group leader, don't spend much time worrying about success or failure. Just getting out on the streets counts as a major success no matter how your outreach project goes. The anointing of the Lord will rest upon those who are willing to take the risk of bringing the love of God to others.

Mistakes are predictable in any new endeavor, but a group outreach helps us to feel less vulnerable. Most of my greatest learning experiences in evangelism have come as I stepped out, and failed, in the safety of a group. My first face-to-face contact with the needy came on Christmas Eve with a small group of five men. I had never actually gone into a poor area to see firsthand how some people live. I had no idea how to proceed. I had never read anything on the subject, but I was willing to step out because I was convinced that God loves the poor. As we draw near to those he particularly wants to reach, we will experience the Holy Spirit empowering us to minister more effectively.

On this particular morning we first gathered for prayer and instruction. One man in the group asked, "Steve, how do you minister to the poor anyway?"

I said, "Just watch me. This is simple."

Sometimes it's best to just step out in boldness. When I knocked on the first door, I heard three deadbolts turn. The woman behind the door peered out through two chains. "Yeah, what do you want?" By this time all four team members were looking over my shoulder, paying close attention to my every word and move. After all, I was the one who said I knew how to minister to the needy.

As we left that home it was difficult to figure out who had been more profoundly touched: the "ministers" in the small group or the family who so joyfully received our food and gifts.

◆◆◆

"We were just wondering, *are you poor?*"

I don't know what got into me. I realize now how incredibly insensitive my words were and I'm still amazed that this woman didn't call the police on us. But in spite of my lack, this woman was touched and unchained the door. With tears in her eyes, she told us her story. Just the night before, she and her five children were praying for God to send them some sort of Christmas. On Christmas Eve, they still had no money for a celebration. The father had taken off with the rent money and was, she suspected, drinking somewhere.

We brought with us an entire Christmas setup—presents for several kids, food, and even a Christmas tree complete with ornaments. As we left that home it was difficult to figure out who had been more profoundly touched: the "ministers" in the small group or the family who so joyfully received our food and gifts.

DISPLAYING THE PEARL

*"One person with a belief is equal to a force of
ninety-nine who only have an interest."*
—John Stuart Mill

*"There was a man, though some did count him mad,
the more he cast away the more he had."*
—John Bunyan

SEVERAL YEARS AGO IN BRAZIL, some children who
were playing in a junkyard found a silver metal
container. Someone cracked it open to reveal the most exquisite
blue, round blob nesting inside. It was different from anything
they'd ever seen. It glowed even in the daylight!

Before long, a crowd had gathered to look at the glowing ball.
Everybody wanted to hold this odd substance. One man dipped
his finger in it and wrote his initials on his bare chest. Another
couple of people played catch with it like it was a rubber ball.
Another man worked the pliable ball into various shapes while
the crowd around him laughed.

Later that day, strange symptoms began to appear on the bodies of all the people who had touched the blue ball. Each person began to feel chilled, feverish, and generally weak. Every bit of skin that had come into contact with this glowing glob had burn marks. Within twenty-four hours the man who had written his initials on his chest had deep burns etched into his skin.

After some investigation it was discovered that the canister had been illegally discarded by a medical equipment company. The contents had at one time been used to save lives by treating cancer. The highly radioactive material was never intended to be touched by human hands. Within a week all of the people who had handled the contents of the canister were dead, victims of radioactive poisoning.

Radioactivity is extremely powerful. In the right environment this power brought life; improperly applied, it can bring great harm and even death. Jesus approached the power of the kingdom of God in similar terms in this parable: "The kingdom of heaven is like a merchant seeking beautiful pearls, who, when he had found one pearl of great price, went and sold all that he had and bought it" (Mt 13:45-46).

Jesus used the rarest pearl to represent the enormous treasure a believer finds in relationship with God. When we experience the goodness of God, we become willing to pay whatever price is necessary to enter into his family. And in repenting and coming to Jesus, we do lose all to find the pearl. As Paul says, we "count all things loss for the excellence of the knowledge of Christ" (Phil 3:8).

It would be unnatural to find the most unusual pearl in the world only to hide it from view. Such a rare treasure is something to get excited about! Who in their right mind would want to keep such a fabulous find to themselves? Those who own much jewelry know that pearls especially need to be worn regularly to keep their luster. If not exposed to fresh air they eventually grow discolored and begin to disintegrate.

Most of you have experienced the awesome beauty of the pearl of which Jesus spoke. Do you know that this pearl, if held onto and not shared, can produce a toxic counterfeit of Christianity? Jesus referred to the Pharisees as "hypocrites," "whitewashed tombs which indeed appear beautiful outwardly, but inside are full of dead men's bones and all uncleanness" (Mt 23:27). These men had hidden the pearl in a cloak of religious rules and regulations so airtight that only the nearly perfect dared come into the temple.

What we do with the pearl of great price reveals our deepest attitudes. If we hold onto it with a stingy heart, the kingdom of heaven can disintegrate around us. If that which was intended to be displayed outwardly is clutched to ourselves, our hearts can suffer spiritual decay and even death.

God's heart has always been inclusive.
He has always provided a place for outsiders
to hear about his mercy.

◆◆◆

Jesus ran into another group of people who were hoarding the pearl (see Jn 2:13-16). If you look in the maps section of your Bible you may find a layout of the temple in Jerusalem. The outermost portion was designated as the "Court of the Gentiles" where non-Jews could hear teaching on the one true God. We can see in this arrangement that God's heart has always been inclusive. He has always provided a place for outsiders to hear about his mercy.

In Jesus' day this area of the temple had been taken over by the religious rulers and designated as a place for exchanging money and selling animals to be used in temple sacrifices. Because of their action, the pearl of great price had been locked away in the temple so that outsiders were excluded from experiencing the grandeur of God's love.

Jesus became furious with these temple leaders. His anger drove him to the point that he expelled the moneychangers from the temple, turned over their tables, and scattered their animals. It seems ironic that the Messiah, the Prince of Peace, expressed such tremendous anger in this particular setting. I believe that Jesus was displaying the heart of God in a way that we've seldom seen. Nothing makes God angrier than people who keep the pearl from being displayed for the world to see.

The cleansing of the temple launched Jesus' public ministry. For the next three years he served with an attitude opposite to that of the excluding temple leaders. Jesus put wheels on the pearl. Wherever he went his goal was to display the glory and majesty of God. The Son of God knew that when outsiders saw the beauty of this divine relationship clearly displayed, they would be attracted to the family of God.

Our call is the same: to take the pearl of great price, attach wheels to it, and take it out into the community. The incarnation manifests this same reality: God coming among humankind. Our tendency to hide this pearl has plagued the church in every generation of believers. Let's see what we can learn by considering a group with passion for God but little practical expression of that life to the world.

THE CHURCH OF LAODICEA: BE HOT OR COLD!

Chapters 2 and 3 of the Revelation of John contain letters to the seven primary churches in what was then called Asia Minor (modern Turkey). These groups were for the most part rebuked for failures in their attitudes. One of them was located in the city of Laodicea, famous around the world for its eye salve. This ointment was highly sought after because it brought welcome relief from eye infections so common in that day.[1] Jesus is referring to this salve when he recommends they take some of their own medicine so that they will be able to see clearly (Rv 3:18).

Two key elements were necessary to produce this salve: very hot and very cold water. In the hills surrounding Laodicea, a natural spring bubbled with both hot and cold water. Their salve put this city on the map, but there was one problem: production was severely limited by their outmoded means of manufacturing. The factory in Laodicea could not keep up with the demand for the famous salve.

The city leaders proposed a plan to upscale their factory and capitalize on the demand for their product. Taxes were increased, private money was invested, and before long, a huge new factory had been built in the center of Laodicea. An elaborate conduit system, considered advanced for that day, transported the hot and cold water right into the factory. At last the grand opening took place and at the big moment the conduits were flooded with water from the hillside springs.

Because of the enormous financial investment, what happened next must have been incredibly anticlimactic. To everyone's shock, the very hot water had cooled down to just lukewarm by the time it flowed into the new factory. The very cold water had warmed up in the conduit to also become just lukewarm. The production process for this eye salve was unforgiving: both very hot and very cold water were absolutely necessary. Now, after such an investment of time and money, all they had was luke-warm water.

In my reading of these seven letters in Revelations, the most striking message is given to the church of Laodicea. If the first six received correction, this last church received a double-barreled rebuke: "I know your works, that you are neither cold nor hot. I wish you were cold or hot. So then, because you are lukewarm, and neither cold nor hot, I will spew you out of my mouth" (Rv 3:15-16).

These words have been often quoted by evangelists as mean-ing, "get hot for God or else!" Or get cold with him, which is to be against him, because it's better to be clearly against God and his kingdom than to play games. Lukewarm is taken to mean hypocrisy—the person who says they belong to Christ but whose life betrays the fact that they really don't. The typical modern interpretation is that we ought to be living a "hot" brand of

Christianity or we will ultimately be vomited from the mouth of God.

◆◆◆

Lukewarmness doesn't mean a lack of excitement or commitment to God, rather it is a void of usefulness. To be lukewarm is to fail at making our Christianity real.

◆◆◆

When John's letter was read by the Laodicean believers, they understood a very different message. "Because you are lukewarm, and neither cold nor hot, I will spew you out of my mouth." The church in Laodicea understood instantly the call of the resurrected Christ. In saying, "I could wish you were cold or hot," Jesus was saying in essence, *be useful* in my kingdom. Both hot and cold were equally useful in the making of eye salve. Lukewarm was totally useless.

Lukewarmness doesn't mean a lack of excitement or commitment to God, rather it is a void of usefulness. To be lukewarm is to fail at making our Christianity real. So what does a useful Christian life look like? A few believers are called to live out their faith as contemplatives who spend the bulk of their time in prayer—an extremely useful vocation in the kingdom of God. Most of us are called to a more action-oriented approach to following Christ.

A pastor friend of mine relayed a story that happened not long ago when he was leading a service project. This group was washing windshields in the parking lot of a grocery store. One clean-cut young guy walked up to a four by four truck with a couple of really rough guys staring at him. With gusto he asked the driver, "How would you like it if I washed your windshield free to show you God's love?"

The man responded back, "How would you like it if I broke your arm to show you God's love? Stay away from my truck!"

The young Christian remained undaunted and answered back, "You don't understand. We're doing this to show you God's love in a way that will meet a need in your life. We're not taking money; we're here because Jesus loves you."

This truck driver didn't quite know how to respond. He just stared for a moment with his mouth agape. He then slowly replied, "Oh, I get it. Two thousand years ago Jesus washed people's feet. Now you're kind of doing the same thing by washing my windshield. Sure, you can wash my windshield."

GONZO CHRISTIANITY

Enormous opportunity stands before us right now, even at our very doorstep. As we uncover the hunger for spiritual reality in America, we can choose to either watch or jump in as "gonzo Christians." Hunter Thompson, one of the most colorful writers alive today, coined the term "gonzo journalism" to describe his unusual approach to covering a news story. Instead of writing from the outside as a neutral observer, Thompson's goal is to cover an event from the inside as a participant. He takes his paper and pencil and jumps into the middle of the crowd.

"Oh, I get it. Two thousand years ago Jesus washed people's feet. Now you're kind of doing the same thing by washing my windshield. Sure, you can wash my windshield."

Today is the day for an army of gonzo Christians to come to the forefront of the church. The days of watching, listening, studying the end times, and arguing our point about when Jesus is *really* coming back are over! This heartfelt desire to win the world for Christ was driven home one morning with a friend of mine while he was jogging. He was running alone, using the time for devotional prayer, telling the Lord how much he loved him, when he sensed the Lord speak to him. The Holy Spirit seemed to say, *"You spend all your time trying to figure out how to get off the earth when I'm trying to get you on the earth!"*

What sorts of attitudes will allow us to be useful in displaying the pearl? As gonzo Christians, we need to be peculiar people willing to take on these same attitudes.

"Greater is he ..." We must make a commitment to take the pearl out to those who live beyond the church walls. We will never succeed unless we believe that "he who is in you is greater than he who is in the world" (1 Jn 4:4). I don't know any Christian who doesn't officially believe that verse, but most believers I know have never put this truth to the test. We will never discover the greatness of him who is in us until we go into the world with the good news. We will never know the greatness of the light unless we shine our light into the surrounding darkness.

For years I kept my goals so small and easily attainable that they didn't require the blessing of God upon them to materialize. Now my desire is to live out a Christian life that requires that "greater than" promise of power. In Cincinnati we are working on an ambitious plan to help start approximately thirty new churches. Last year our network of churches touched approximately five hundred thousand people with deeds of practical love.

I believe that we will see a day in the near future when various fellowships around the city will have mobilized enough to touch one-tenth of the city each year. Over a several year period we will be able to reach most of this city with acts of love and charity. And what is going on in Cincinnati could be done in every city in the country.

A friend of mine pastors an evangelical church in Fort Collins, Colorado. His church has mobilized about one hundred people who go into the community about once a month doing deeds of kindness. That group of one hundred could easily touch half of their city each year with the love of God. It won't take long for them to literally saturate their city with deeds of love. Pretty soon they'll be known all over town as "the people who serve others."

Reckless abandon to the cause of Christ. Several years ago I saw a movie called *Red Dawn,* a thought-provoking film though probably a bit reactionary. The story follows the exploits of a band of high schoolers who are trying to survive a foreign invasion of their Colorado town. Overnight they must make the transformation from being self-centered teenagers into being soldiers who survive against the toughest odds.

Although reckless at first, bit by bit they grow smarter and stronger until they eventually take on entire enemy battalions with ease. The key for these high schoolers is their willingness to take risks. They realize that most of the important lessons of warfare are learned in the wake of disaster.

In just the same way, we must be willing to grow in our ministry skill as we go along. The key in servant evangelism is to just get started. If we demand a risk-free brand of Christianity, we certainly won't grow and we won't be effective in reaching the world around us. Those who claim to be ministry experts and haven't yet experienced significant failure scare me. I don't trust them because I know that risk and pain accompany any significant progress in reaching out with the good news of Jesus Christ.

The key in servant evangelism is to just get started.
If we demand a risk-free brand of Christianity,
we certainly won't grow and we won't be effective
in reaching the world around us.

Luke explains that his gospel account told the story of "all that Jesus *began* both to do and teach" (Acts 1:1). Jesus launched his ministry, which was then carried on by the church which he instituted. Their call was to do the works of Jesus—to feed, clothe, visit, give cold water, speak the truth, give encouragement. Jesus tells a parable in Matthew 25 about two groups of people—which he calls sheep and goats—who were being tested. Neither of them knew they were encountering Jesus when they saw the needy. He praises the sheep who did the works of compassion and kindness; he reprimands and punishes the goats who did not do those works.

We identify ourselves as either sheep or goats by the way we respond to the hurting around us. Fourteen years ago I met a group of about ten Christians who had gathered together out of a desire to reach the community in practical ways with the mercy, grace, and love of God. It was exciting for me to be with them because they were open to doing whatever it would take to accomplish their goal.

My encouragement to them was to first get a feel for the needs of the people of their city. They needed to begin to ask themselves, "Where in our city would a helping hand, a free bag of groceries, a timely coin in a parking meter, or a cold drink make a difference?" Squeaky wheels can be found all around us if we would just listen.

This small group took my counsel and eagerly began to develop a strategy for reaching out to the unchurched. They weren't satisfied with just inviting people to meetings. Before long they had provided food for single moms, sponsored a major clothing drive for needy school children, given away free school supplies, put on language clinics for immigrants, and offered financial counseling to those in economic difficulties. They began to bring the kingdom out into the community.

I have had only occasional contact with this group for the past several years and haven't really functioned in any coaching capacity with them. When I spoke there on a Sunday morning, I was amazed to see what the Lord has been doing in their midst. These people have really been doing the works of the sheep! They have grown in just four years to the largest church in town with over seven hundred members. People are coming to Christ regularly. They've started another church in a nearby city, with plans to start two more in the next two years. Equally exciting to me are the numbers of people in the community who are being touched with kindness and the number of Christians who want to continue reaching out with the mercy, grace, and love of God.

PAVING A ROAD OF LOVE AND ACCEPTANCE

One Labor Day we held a free car wash. We have tried car washes at different locations—gas stations, malls, grocery stores, and even bank parking lots on holidays. Our favorite spot is a place on the north side of Cincinnati called Jenny's Sportsbar. Best known for their country music and "meanest man" contests, this bar advertises on several popular FM radio stations.

We had washed several dozen cars on this particular day when a man cruised in at the wheel of a flashy new import. He hopped out of the car and we went to work. As the "designated evangelist" at the moment, I began to explain why we were washing his car for free. This man smiled, nodded in approval, and then said, "So who do I make out my check to?"

"You don't understand, sir. We aren't taking money for this car wash. We just want to show you God's love in a practical way," I said. I repeated this explanation three times before he finally got it. I could tell because his expression changed: he lit up, his eyes got big, and his mouth was hanging open. By my fourth explanation, he was all ears.

Then he did something that I have seen several times when doing servant evangelism. This man began to confess his failures to me right there in the parking lot of Jenny's Sportsbar. He told me about his sexual escapades, his lack of church attendance, and yet his awareness of God's presence over the years. He told me that he had been a starting pitcher for a National League baseball team until suffering a career-ending knee injury.

This was an amazing turn of events. In just a couple of minutes, I had encountered this man at a very deep level. He had just shared several intimate secrets of his heart with a total stranger.

Our kindness had paved a road of love and acceptance for this man. His response spoke of a sincere desire to reconnect with this God who had taken time to seek him out.

There is only one more thing you need to do to join God's conspiracy of kindness. Put this book down, pick up a squeegee, and start washing windshields.

There is only one more thing you need to do to join God's conspiracy of kindness. Put this book down, pick up a squeegee, and start washing windshields. I would enjoy sharing more with you about bringing God's love to your community, but I've run out of time. In five minutes I'm meeting some friends to go and wash windshields at a grocery store parking lot. If you were here I'd offer you a squeegee and have you come along. We'd have great fun!

Epilogue

When *Conspiracy of Kindness* came out ten years ago, I had no idea that it would have the staying power it has turned out to have. Apparently kindness is doable! I have been thrilled to write another seven books—all on the topic of kindness! (You can check these out at my website at www.servantevangelism.com.)

The concept of kindness opening the door to the heart seems to be a universal human truth. I have traveled through much of the world since *Conspiracy* was published (by the way, it has come out in a number of languages). All indications are that people are universally vulnerable to the power of the kindness of God: "The kindness of God leads to repentance" (Rom 2:4.)

I have learned a handful of lessons these past few years since *Conspiracy* first came out.

1. **Faithfulness counts.** Keep on keeping on in your acts of generosity no matter what the outcome seems at first. Usually the first attempt to serve one's way into the community is a slow start. In fact, in my experience, it takes about two years for the first people who are served to steadily make their way into church. But no matter! Your church will grow in the meantime just the same because you will be manifesting a winsomeness to your city that is very attractive.

2. **"Small things done with great love will change the world."** I have given up on trying to do big things for God. I've come to this conclusion: all that counts is our attempts at small things done with faithfulness to God over the long haul. When we attempt to do big things for God, more often than not we end up bringing glory to ourselves and that not only doesn't count for God, it also looks ridiculous.

3. **There are unlimited creative ways to share the love of Christ.** Here in Cincinnati, just when we think, "Now that's the best idea we've had yet!" someone comes along with another idea that is even more creative. If you are a regular visitor to our website, you will notice that we are coming up with new projects continually. People from all over the world are coming up with new ways to bring the love of Christ to their culture. I encourage you—get with your fellow "s.e." friends over a cup of coffee on a regular basis and let your imaginations run wild by the power of the Holy Spirit.

4. **Just a few people can make a big difference.** It seems that all significant movements start with a small minority. Almost everywhere I go, I see servant evangelism start with a small group of people who are willing to roll up their sleeves and get some dirt under their fingernails. Kindness is contagious. Small groups grow into large groups in time. Don't worry about your beginnings.

Recently what started out as a few people in Cincinnati grew to more over the next few months. By the time we had planned our one-day event for several months, we had enlisted some 300 churches. In just a couple of hours we reached out to over 300,000 people.

Focus on your goal—to touch and change your city with the love of Christ!

Steve Sjogren
Cincinnati, Ohio
Winter, 2003

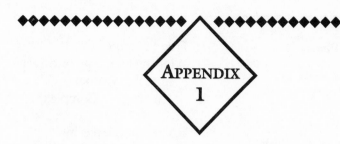

SERVANT EVANGELISM PROJECTS THAT WORK

"If there is any kindness I can show, or any good thing I can do to any fellow being, let me do it now, and not deter or neglect it, as I shall not pass this way again."
—William Penn

All projects are free—no donations accepted!

Some services are provided while those being served are away, making cards or printed notes necessary.

Public Places
(gas stations, restaurants, malls, groceries, retail stores, soccer and baseball fields, etc.)

Umbrella Escorts
Windshield Washing
Coffee Giveaways
Gift Wrapping at Christmas
Soft Drink Giveaways
Restroom Cleaning
Grocery Bag Loading
    Assistance
Bag Packing at Self-Serve
    Groceries
Grocery Cart Return

Sporting Events
Giveaway…Cokes
    Coffee
    Popcorn
    Popsicles
    Peanuts
    Sunglasses (cheap ones)
Windshield Washing

Automobiles
Check Oil and Fill
Single Mom's Oil Change
Washer Fluid Fill
Tire Pressure Check
Windshield Washing at Self-
    Serve Stations
Oil and Filter Change
Interior Vacuuming
Bulb Replacement
Car Wash

Free Fragrance Cards
Windshield Scrape or Sweep
    in Cold Weather
    (Apartment Complex)

Roadside/Drive-by
Summer Car Washes
Coke Giveaways
Winter Car
    Washes/Desalting
Popsicle Giveaways

Downtown/Business Districts
Windshield Washing
Umbrella Escort
Business Window Washing
Toilet Scrubbing
Soft Drink Giveaways
Free Cookies
Free Cappuccino
Feeding Parking Meters
Free Polaroid Photos at
    Carriage Rides
Free Shoe Shine

Parks
Doggie Clean-up
Helium Balloons for Kids
Polaroid Picture Giveaways
Popsicle Giveaways
Grilling Hot Dogs/Free
    Picnic
Gatorade at Biking Trails
Gatorade at Jogging Trails
Pictionary in the Park

Flower Seed Packets
Face Painting

College Campuses
Pen/Pencil Giveaways
Free Copies
Free Coffee, Soft Drinks
Dorm Cleaning
Free Tutoring
Gatorade or Lemonade in
Hot Weather
Hot Chocolate in Cold
Weather
Drink Giveaways at
Intramural Events and
Greek Sports Events
Breakfast Bagels or Pop Tarts

House to House
Leaf Raking
Lawn Mowing
Grass Edging
Screen Cleaning
General Yard Cleanup
Door to Door Carnation
Giveaways
Potted Plant Giveaways
Flower Seed Packet
Giveaways
Gutter Cleaning
Sidewalk Sweeping
Windshield Washing (Car in
Driveway)
Sunday Morning Paper and
Coffee Giveaways

Snow Removal from Walks
and Drives
Empty Garbage Can Return
Kitchen Cleanup
Window Washing
Minor House Repairs
General Cleaning (Interior)
House Number Painting on
Curbs
Free Community Dinner
Doggie Yard Cleanup
Light Bulb Replacement
Minor Tree Trimming
Weed Spraying/Pulling
Seal Blacktop Driveways
Scrape Fireplaces
Radon Detectors
Carbon Monoxide
Detectors
Smoke Detector Batteries
Fragrance Spraying
Filter Change AC/Heat
Garage Cleaning
Free Fireplace Kindling
Bark and Mulch for Yards

Miscellaneous
Mother's Day Carnation
Giveaways
Food Delivery to Shut-ins
Car Drying at Self-Serve Car
Washes
Grocery Store Bag Packing
Free Bird Feeders and Refills
to Convalescent Hospital
Patients

Collect Trees after Christmas for Disposal

Free Bait at Local Fishing Spots

Free Coffee at a Major Bus or Subway Stop

Birthday Party Organizing

Pay Washer and Dryer at Laundromat

Memorial Service

Free Carnation to Cemetery Visitors

Easter Basket Giveaway

Pizza on Moving Day at Apartment or Condo

Lawn Mower Tune-up Clinic

Time Change Reminder Flyer

The options are limitless....
Use your imagination!

Business cards with at least your church or organization's name, address, and phone number are highly recommended at all service projects, so that people will be able to contact you if they need you in the future. A sample of what we use is listed below:

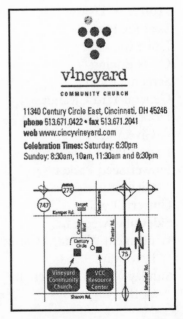

Project	Concept	Equipment	People Needed	Cost	Weather
Single Mom's Free Oil Change	Most single moms have car problems regularly	Cards, * Filters, Oil	5 or more	About $5-$7 per car. Need to give advance notice	Any weather except extreme cold
Neighborhood Windshield Washing	Going door to door washing windshields in driveways	Cards, squeegees, squirt bottles, cleaner, shop rags	2 or more	Minimal	Cool to warm, but not hot
Mother's Day Carnation Giveaway	Set up outside grocery store on Saturday before Mother's Day	Cards, table, "Free Carnations" sign, cards explaining Mother's Day outreach	5 or more	If you order carnations in advance, you will save significantly	
Sunday Morning Paper and Coffee Giveaway	Going door to door early in the morning to houses without a paper in the driveway	Cards, Sunday papers, Igloos of coffee, cups	2 or more	Papers in bulk cost about $1 each	Anything but rain
Snow Removal from Driveways and Sidewalks	Help people dig out of the snow	Cards, shovels, Igloo of coffee, cups	4 or more	Minimal	Snow

Project	Concept	Equipment	People Needed	Cost	Weather
Pulling out Cars Stuck in the Snow	Rescue people from ditches, etc.	Cards, shovels, chains, bag of grit or salt pellets, Igloo of coffee, cups	4 or more per vehicle	Minimal	Snow
Empty Garbage Can Return from Street	Bring cans back to people's houses or garages	Cards	2 or more	None	Any weather
Kitchen Cleanup	Humbling but powerful service	Cards, basic cleaning equipment	2 or more	Minimal	Any weather
Food Delivery to Shut-Ins	Delivering food	Cards	2 or more	None	Any weather
Car Drying at Self-Serve Car Washes	Help dry off cars after they have been washed	Cards, towels or a couple of good chamois	2 or more	Minimal	Car washing weather

Project	Concept	Equipment	People Needed	Cost	Weather
Leaf Raking	Who likes to rake leaves? We do it for them.	Cards, rakes, bags. Blowers work well but they are more expensive.	As few as 2—the more the merrier and easier. 10 people can rake a lawn in minutes.	Minimal—you can own your own rake for $.3.98	About any type, but it's tough raking leaves in wet weather
Christmas Gift Wrap	Everyone needs their Christmas gifts wrapped. Do it at the mall for free!	Cards, wrapping paper, tape, scissors, etc. Build simple kiosk or booth. For suppliers call 513-671-0422	Lots of people needed. Depending upon mall traffic, you will need a variety. Use 3-10/shift	Though costly, can cost as little as $.10/ gift with the right suppliers. Scissors, etc. can be used again	If wrapping at an inside location, weather not a problem
Lawn Care	Find unkept lawns and go for it.	Cards; can do basic mowing or more, depending on your desire (edging, trimming, etc.)	2 or more	Cost of gasoline, oil, and bags	It's easier to mow dry grass than wet grass
Coke Giveaway	On a hot day, nothing refreshes like a cold drink in Jesus' name.	Cards, drinks, ice, clean plastic trash cans for storing cans on ice, table	Minimum of 10	Can lower cost to about $.10/unit buying in quantities. We give out 400+ drinks. Ice varies	Warm or hot weather
Free Coffee	Set up tables at store exits or sporting events and serve hot coffee on cold days.	Cards, table, 2 or 3 Igloos (5 gal.), creamers, sugar, stirrers, cups, sign–"Free Coffee"	3 or more	Minimal	Cool or cold weather

PROJECT	CONCEPT	EQUIPMENT	PEOPLE NEEDED	COST	WEATHER
Popsicle Giveaway	Set up tables at store exits or sporting events and serve popsicles on warm days.	Cards, table, 2-3 Igloos, ice, sign, Popsicles	3 or more	Minimal	Warm weather
Windshield Washing	Hit every car in the lot at stores and shopping centers	Squeegees, squirt bottles with window cleaner, red shop rags, cards**	1 or more. It's more fun with more people	Minimal	Does not work well in weather over 75 degrees—the liquid evaporates too quickly
Grocery Store Bag Packing	Go to a self-bagging grocery store and help people bag their groceries	Cards, might wear matching aprons, button—"just because ..."	2 or more	No cost	Good inclement weather project
Pictionary in the Park	Start playing Pictionary and strangers just show up	Cards, white board & markers, Pictionary cards	5 or more	Minimal	Warm weather—spring or summer
Balloon Giveaway	Go to a park and give balloons and cards to children with parents	Cards, helium tanks, balloons	2 or more	Balloons & helium are about $.10-$.15 per child	Any weather when people are at the park

PROJECT	CONCEPT	EQUIPMENT	PEOPLE NEEDED	COST	WEATHER
Free Bird Feeders to Convalescent Hospitals	Share God's love with shut-ins	Cards, bird feeders, birdseed	2 or more	Birdseed, initial investment in feeders	Any weather, greatest appeal in winter
Free House-Number Painting on Curbs	Address numbers painted on the curb	Cards, stencils, spray paint	2 or more	$1-$2 per house	Dry and warm
Free Community Dinner	Throw a party for a neighborhood	Cards, food	15 or more	Depending on meal choice, $2-$5 per person	Any weather
Coffee Giveaway at a Major Bus Stop	On cold days people enjoy hot coffee.	Cards, coffee, cups, 2 Igloos, condiments	5 or more	Minimal	Cool or cold weather
Free Polaroid Pictures at Horse Carriage Stands	Set up shop at a downtown horse-drawn carriage stand.	Cards, cameras, film	2 or more	About $.75 per picture	Cool to cold; fall and winter weather most popular

PROJECT	CONCEPT	EQUIPMENT	PEOPLE NEEDED	COST	WEATHER
Shopping Assistance for Shut-Ins	Shop for those that can't get out on their own	Cards, vehicles	2 or more	Minimal	Any weather
Collect Trees after Christmas for Proper Disposal	Meet a practical clean-up need	Cards, vehicles	2 or more	None	Any weather
Doggie Dirt Cleanup of Neighborhood Yards	Clean up doggie mess	Cards, pooper scooper or use plastic bags over hands, bags	2 or more	Minimal	Any weather; very cold is easiest
Shoe Shining Service	Free shoe shining at stores, malls, other public places	Cards, shoe polish, rags (kits are great)	2 or more	Initial investment minimal	Not a factor if done indoors
Feeding Parking Meters	Find expired parking meters before cars are ticketed and leave a note of explanation	Cards, lots of change	2 or more	You can feed a lot of parking meters for $20	Not a factor except for extreme conditions

PROJECT	CONCEPT	EQUIPMENT	PEOPLE NEEDED	COST	WEATHER
Light Bulb Service	Go door to door with light bulbs offering to change burned-out bulbs	Supply 15-60 watt light bulbs, cards, step ladder	Teams of 2	Light bulbs are $.30 to $.50 apiece	
Laundromat Outreach	Pay for washing machines and dryers at local laundromats	Cards, rolls of dimes or quarters	Teams of 2—women do best at this—intimidating to have more than a few people	At least $1.50 per wash, $.25 per dryer	
Blood Pressure Screening	Check people's blood pressure at public places	Cards, stethoscopes, sphygmomanometers	Teams of 2-4 work well	Initial investment necessary, many nurses have own equipment	
Car Safety Light Check	Replace burned-out bulbs in cars	Cards, variety of spare bulbs to replace burn-outs, screwdrivers	Teams of 2-4	Replacement bulbs vary in price	Dry weather best
Killing Weeds	Spray for weeds and poison ivy on sidewalks, driveways, etc.	Cards, weed killer, sprayers, gloves, masks	Teams of 2-4	Weed killer varies; least expensive in gallons and dilute into sprayers	Warm, dry; ideally in summer

PROJECT	CONCEPT	EQUIPMENT	PEOPLE NEEDED	COST	WEATHER
Seal Blacktop Driveways	Help homeowners seal driveways—best to use flyers to stimulate interest	Cards, sealer, sealer brooms	Teams of 4-6	Costs vary	Any weather
House Gutter Cleaning	Clean gutters on houses of leaves, sticks, and debris	Cards, gloves, ladders, trash bags	Teams of 2-4. Everyone needs a ladder	Plastic bags ongoing after ladders are purchased	Dry weather best
Birthday Party Organizing	Organize and run parties for children—advertise in local papers	Cards, music for party	2-4 Clowns	Parents pay for supplies, ads in free and local papers are best	
Door-to-Door Food Collection for the Poor	Put out flyers door to door then return a week later to pick up cans and dry goods and deliver to poor	Cards, bags given out	Teams of 2	Purchase bags	Not a factor
Car Interior Vacuuming	Set up in mall parking lot or at gas station and vacuum cars	Cards, several canister vacuums, several hand-held vacuums	Teams of 4+	Nothing to purchase if using home vacuum cleaners	Dry weather is best

PROJECT	CONCEPT	EQUIPMENT	PEOPLE NEEDED	COST	WEATHER
Filling Windshield Washer Fluid in Cars	Refill washer reserves in cars and clean off wiper blades	Cards, washer fluid, signs, table	4-10 on a team	Fluid commonly costs about $1.00 per gallon	Any weather
Cleaning Fireplaces	Remove ashes	Cards, small brooms, small flat shovels	Teams of 2	Purchase trash bags, possible initial investment on tools	Usually a cool weather project.
Checking Air on Tires	See if tires are properly inflated—adjust pressure if necessary	Cards, compressor or portable air "bubbles," air pressure gauges	Teams of 4-6	Pressure gauges not much, borrow compressors or air tanks	Almost any weather but people are more concerned in summer
Memorial Service	Advertise complimentary memorial service in newspaper or telephone book	Cards	Pastor and others to set up and take down	Advertising	
Radon Detectors	Give out complimentary detectors in areas where radon is a concern. Return in a few days.	Cards, detectors	Teams of 2	In quantity these cost about $10.00 each	

PROJECT	CONCEPT	EQUIPMENT	PEOPLE NEEDED	COST	WEATHER
Carbon Monoxide Detectors	Give out complimentary carbon monoxide detectors. Come back in a few days to check	Cards, detectors	Teams of 2	In quantity these cost about $3.50 each	Usually a winter project
Smoke Detector Batteries	Give out complimentary smoke detector batteries for refills	Cards—reminders with date, batteries	Teams of 2	In quantity these cost about $1.25 per battery	Any weather
Toilet Cleaning	Clean toilets of restaurants and stores	Cards, urinal screens, cleaning supplies	Teams of 2	Supply costs vary—minimal	Any weather
Outdoor Window Washing	Wash first floor windows	Cards, professional squeegees and cleaner, short ladder, buckets	2 or more	One time purchase of squeegees—not too expensive	50 degrees or more
Yard Cleanup	Look for messy yards	Cards, trash bags, rakes	2 or more	Minimal	

PROJECT	CONCEPT	EQUIPMENT	PEOPLE NEEDED	COST	WEATHER
Easter Basket Giveaway	Every child wants an Easter Basket	Cards, baskets vary. We put in candy, Christian literature. Once we put in Christian tapes	2 or more	Costs vary from $3 to $5 per basket	
Rainy Day Grocery Escort	Help shoppers to cars with packages	Cards, golf umbrellas	2 or more	Minimal	Rainy days
Polaroid Pictures	Find lonely people or couples at parks or malls and "shoot" them	Cameras, cards, (stickers for back of photo are best)	2 or more	Film & initial outlay for cameras. (About $.75 per photo)	
Windshield Washing at Self-Serve Gas Station	Revive the practice of free windshield washing with fill-up	Cards, squeegees, squirt bottles, red rags, cleaner	2 or more	Initial purchase of equipment—minimal	Prefer clear weather. If it's too hot the cleaner will evaporate
House/Apartment Repair	Fix broken things. Limit repairs to your capabilities	Cards, basic tool kit	2 or more *capable* repair people. Don't send unskilled—they can make things worse.	Limit your work to your budget. We do a lot of winterizing at a low cost	

Project	Concept	Equipment	People Needed	Cost	Weather
House/Apartment/Dorm Cleaning	Who *doesn't* need housework help?	Cards, vacuum cleaners, brooms, trash bags	2 or more	Minimal	Any weather—may need to call ahead or work from referrals
Winter Car Wash	Spray off salt and road grime	Cards, coffee supplies, wands to spray off underside of cars	10 or more	Minimal	Don't attempt this in weather below 20 degrees—could freeze door locks
Summer Car Wash	Free car wash! We use banners that say "Free Car Wash—No Kidding"	Cards, basic wash equipment, banners. Can also serve drinks, play music, provide lawn chairs.	Minimum of 12/prefer 25-30. We do 2-3 cars at once. Designate an "evangelist" to talk to people	Minimal—We often use a sports bar's parking lot and pay for the water.	Above 60 degrees. Overcast days don't work well. People won't stop if it looks like rain.

*Cards should have your fellowship name, phone, meeting time(s), and an easy-to-follow map on back.
**This card reads: "While you were away from your car, people from the Vineyard Christian Fellowship washed your windshield."

APPENDIX 2

EVANGELISM ASSUMPTIONS

by Doug Murren, Doug Roe, and Steve Sjogren

Let these statements help you step out with confidence into service evangelism.

1. Deep down non-Christians really want to know and obey God.
2. Non-Christians typically have five or more significant encounters with the gospel before coming into a relationship with Jesus Christ.
3. Non-Christians usually won't come to us to find God. We have to go to them.
4. Evangelism is the easiest and most natural of all the ministries in the church.
5. Effective evangelism requires little training.
6. Friendly, openhearted people make the best evangelists.
7. Church life, spent in the presence of Christians only, produces saints who are neither friendly nor openhearted to outsiders.

8. The kingdom of God is the primary mission and issue of our shared life as Christians, not self-preservation or the perpetuation of a church.

9. The primary foundation of all our evangelism is love.

10. Placing expectations upon someone we're evangelizing is always injurious and works against that person coming to Christ.

11. We become holy and righteous by identifying with Jesus and surrendering to his will for us rather than trying to obey the law.

12. Each person in relationship with Jesus is primarily responsible for his or her own follow-up and fellowship needs.

13. The Holy Spirit is the only true evangelist who has ever existed, as well as the only disciple-maker.

14. It is normal for everyone who loves Jesus to have a heart for the poor, sick, lost, widowed, and homeless.

15. We are committed to prayer as an essential element of any successful outreach venture. Because we highly value active obedience to the will of God, an ideal time to pray is on the way to share God's love with others.

16. Non-Christians may not remember what they've been told regarding God's love, but they always remember what they've experienced of God's love.

17. None of us can manufacture the genuine working of the Holy Spirit.

18. The Holy Spirit is able, willing, and free to break in and carry on his work in unspectacular, non-manipulative, and surprising ways.

19. An atmosphere of anointing, freshness, and vitality comes upon believers when they spend time with non-Christians.

20. Because of irrational fears, the average evangelical Christian today has no plans to participate actively in evangelism.

21. Most Christians are so far out of touch with the world around them that they know little of its fears, problems, concerns, or issues.

22. Because God is highly committed to the lost, almost any evangelistic approach will work given enough time and commitment to sharing the good news.

23. God has a passionate heart for the lost. Whether we choose to bring Christ to unbelievers or not, God is very creative and will always seek to win them in some way.

24. It is a privilege to be involved in the process of sharing God's love with those he is inviting into the family of God.

25. Effective evangelism is more of a mindset and paradigm than a program.

26. Our evangelism is really an overflow of our relationship with God and our relationships with people.

27. In order to effectively evangelize our cities, we will need to make major time commitments to sharing our lives with the lost. In fact, God may ask us to dedicate the rest of our lives to the task of reaching our cities with the gospel.

28. The value of evangelism will regularly conflict with day to day programs of church life.

29. Because they are central to the mission of the local church, funding for evangelism and ministry to the poor ought to be seen as a part of the regular church budget rather than areas to be financed by special offerings.

RECOMMENDED READING

Aldrich, Joe. *Gentle Persuasion*. Portland, Ore.: Multnomah, 1988. Aldrich speaks from his many years of experience as a friendship evangelist. He has done an outstanding job of maintaining relationships with not-yet Christians while working in the ministry—something not many pastors manage to do. His enthusiasm is contagious.

Cook, Jerry, with Stanley C. Baldwin. *Love, Acceptance and Forgiveness*. Ventura, Calif.: Regal, 1979. I consider this a modern-day classic work on the application of God's grace to the daily Christian life. The principles Cook presents will cause you to examine your own church's way of approaching outsiders.

Dennison, Jack. *City Reaching*. Pasadena, Calif., William Carey Publishing, 1999. This is one of the most exciting books that I've read in the past several years. Dennison presents a bold and hopeful view for the Church's future, but not one that will be free from radically different ways of doing things. I especially resonated with his vision for church planting.

Erwin, Gayle D. *The Jesus Style.* Waco, Tex.: Word, 1983. Erwin convincingly presents the life of Jesus as one of supreme servanthood. This book will make you uncomfortable unless you are willing to take one giant step forward in serving others. I would put it at the top of my list of books related to servant evangelism.

Gerber, Michael. *The E Myth.* New York: Ballinger-Harper & Row, 1986. Anyone involved in a growing ministry that is innovative will find this a very helpful treatment on the misunderstandings common among entrepreneurs.

Kawasaki, Guy. *Selling the Dream.* New York: Harper Collins, 1991. As a former "software evangelist" for Apple computers, Kawasaki explored the implications of selling a new idea. Many of his ideas carry over to Christian evangelism. Part of his discovery process included attending the Billy Graham School of Evangelism.

Ladd, George E. *The Gospel of the Kingdom.* Grand Rapids, Mich.: Eerdmans, 1959. Ladd's insights into the presences of the kingdom of God have had an enormous impact on evangelicals over the past thirty years, and have specifically influenced the development of my thinking as I developed servant evangelism.

Lewis, Robert. *The Church of Irresistible Influence.* Grand Rapids, Mich.: Zondervan, 2001. Lewis and his church in Little Rock have taken the basic idea of servant evangelism and run with it. They have taken on large projects on a city-wide level such as rehabbing schools. After doing these projects for years now they have seen amazing results and have developed great influence in the community and state.

Little, Paul. *How to Give Away Your Faith.* Downers Grove, Ill.: InterVarsity Press, 1966. Little's book has helped many fearful Christians step into the arena of evangelism over the past several decades. It continues to prove itself a classic.

McLaren, Brian D. *Finding Faith.* Grand Rapids, Mich.: Zondervan, 2000. There are lots of evidences that our culture is very interested in spiritual things. That perspective is one that sometimes runs counter to the popular opinion of the Church. Written in the tradition of C.S. Lewis in *Mere Christianity* and Scott Peck's *The Road Less Traveled*, this book challenges the reader to think in terms more of how one believes more than what one believes. A great book for bridging the gap with not-yet Christians.

McLaren, Brian D. *More Ready Than You Realize.* Grand Rapids, Mich.: Zondervan, 2002. How open to God are not-yet believers to begin to follow God in a personal way? McLaren argues that they are more open than most Christians tend to think. We have simply tended to put seekers into categories that fit our mental frameworks nicely, but don't do them a lot of good. He compares the approach to coming to Christ to a dance between the church and the unchurched. Reading this will make you eager to go to the dance.

McManus, Erwin R. *An Unstoppable Force: Daring to Become the Church God Had in Mind.* Loveland, Colo.: Group, 2001. What would happen if God actually got his way with the church? McManus ponders that question and comes up with some thoughts about the church that are exciting and challenging. Don't read this one unless you are ready for your view of the church to be rocked a bit.

Mittelberg, Mark & Bill Hybles. *Building a Contagious Church.* Grand Rapids, Mich.: Zondervan, 2000. Here are principles and proven practices from historic Willow Creek Church on how to build a church atmosphere that is truly contagious. Mittelberg speaks from the accrued experience of years of living this stuff out in Chicago.

Ortiz, Juan Carlos. *Disciple.* Lake Mary, Fla.: Creation House, 1975. This is a refreshing little book that is very helpful to new believers. It has helped many thousands of Christians find their way forward into a simple, childlike Christianity that emphasizes obedience.

Pippert, Rebecca Manley. *Out of the Saltshaker & Into the World.* Downers Grove, Ill.: InterVarsity Press, 1979. Pippert confesses to being a timid evangelist. Her quotable line is, "Only two groups struggle with evangelism: Christians and non-Christians." She gives encouragement for Christians to form and maintain significant relationships with those not yet in Christ. She offers principles for personal evangelism that are timeless and golden. This book is essential for your library.

Random Acts of Kindness, a compilation, Berkeley, Calif.: Conari, 1993. Though not a "Christian" book, this compilation of stories gives testimony to the power of kindness in the lives of many. Many ideas are shared for meeting needs in others' lives. Some of them are practical and easily adaptable to servant evangelism.

Roxburgh, Alan J. *The Missionary Congregation, Leadership, and Liminality.* Harrisburg, Penn.: Trinity Press International, 1997. In this small book author Roxburgh explains that the modern church has been pushed into a chaplain's role in society. He offers no easy answers to the matters we face, but concludes that we must become missionary congregations emerging into the world. A very thought-provoking, helpful book.

Scazzero, Pete. *Introducing Jesus.* Downers Grove, Ill.: InterVarsity Press, 1991. The author of many popular study guides, Scazzero offers us many insights into sharing Christ with friends and family. He writes with authority and fire as an effective personal evangelist who has had fruitful ministry for years.

Sjogren, Steve. *101 Ways to Reach Your Community.* Colorado Springs, Colo.: NavPress, 2001. This is a follow-up to *Conspiracy of Kindness.* It is a virtual cookbook of outreach projects that are laid out in simple, moderate, and more complex projects. All that is needed for each project is clearly spelled out. This is a great resource for small groups who have gotten the basic idea of servant evangelism down and are ready to go for it.

Sjogren, Steve and Janie. *101 Ways to Reach Those in Need.* Colorado Springs, Colo.: NavPress, 2002. Similar to the above guidebook, this one is directed to those who are interested in specifically reaching out to the needy. It contains a lot of practical tips on how to begin to minister to the needy and assumes the reader is starting out with little or no experience. The projects are varied and creative. Both of these books can be ordered at the servant evangelism website (www.servantevangelism.com) or by toll-free phone at 888.KINDNESS.

Sweet, Leonard. *Aquachurch*. Loveland, Colo.: Group, 2000. Sweet is simply the foremost interpreter of our culture in the Church today. I buy all of his books because his insights on postmodernity are so sharp. *Aquachurch* argues that the Church exists in a time and place of flux and we need to be ready to flow with the changing times around us if we hope to have any impact.

Wimber, John, with Kevin Springer. *Power Evangelism*. San Francisco: Harper & Row, 2000. Wimber has helped many Christians see ministry in a new way. *Power Evangelism* will challenge you to examine your own assumptions about evangelism.

Endorsements

"For ten years, *Conspiracy of Kindness* has been spiritual leaven in the church. *Conspiracy of Kindness* has worked its way into the heart and life of the American church, stimulating the release of God's grace and love. *Conspiracy of Kindness* is more than theory. Conspiracy means 'to breathe with,' and Steve Sjogren's book has indeed started a conspiracy by assisting the church to partner with the Spirit to breathe out the love of God into a world that desperately needs to know God's love.

Bert Waggoner
National Director, Vineyard-USA
Senior Pastor, Vineyard Church, Sugar Land, Texas

"Steve Sjogren's *Conspiracy of Kindness* has made a great contribution to churches everywhere that wanted to reach out but needed new ways to do it and new ways to involve people who had never reached out before. The fact that 'servant evangelism' was modeled through his Cincinnati Vineyard church grounds the book in reality, and the book's many examples give us viable options. This book has awakened the entrepreneurial spirit in some churches, who then invented outreach ministries that Steve never thought of! This new edition assures the book's continued influence."

George Hunter
School of World Mission and Evangelism
Asbury Theological Seminary

"Do you like the idea of reaching people for Christ, but fear the process? In this straightforward and powerful book, Steve Sjogren presents practical ideas every one of us can use. The results can be dramatic—and have an impact for all of eternity. So read the book, join the conspiracy, roll up your sleeves, and watch God work!"

Mark Mittleberg
Author of *Building a Contagious Church*
Evangelism Leader for the Willow Creek Association

"This classic book leads us into non-threatening love actions that release the power of the gospel to transform lives forever."

Dale Galloway
Dean, The Beeson International Center
Asbury Theological Seminary

"In *Conspiracy of Kindness*, the genius of Steve Sjogren shines. He gives readers an uncomplicated, fun way to get the whole church doing evangelism. Steve shows us how to lower the 'E-word' hurdle so that even those who don't have 'the gift of evangelism' can participate. I'm telling you it's genius...."

Todd Hunter
Past National Director Vineyard-USA
Executive Director Allelon Church Planting Foundation

"*Conspiracy of Kindness* explains one of the absolute best biblical methods of reaching out to the unconnected without any trace of bigotry or superiority."

Bill Easum
President, Easum, Bandy & Associates (www.easumbandy.com)

"Steve Sjogren makes it both practical and enjoyable simply to be kind. What a refreshing approach to expressing the love of God to everyday people."

Dudley Hall
Author and President of the Fellowship of Connected Churches and Ministries

"Most Christians become paralyzed just thinking about evangelism. But relax! Steve Sjogren will show you how to demonstrate God's love in practical ways. It's so easy, you will be motivated and equipped to join with other believers in the conspiracy of kindness."

Robert E. Logan
Founder of CoachNet
Coauthor of *Releasing Your Church's Potential*

"There are two things I especially love about servant evangelism: first, what it does for those who are served, showing them a kind face of Christianity (as opposed to an angry or argumentative face), and second, what it does for those who serve. It builds in them an identity as servants, which I think must make Jesus smile. May the conspiracy of kindness spread!"

Brian McLaren
Pastor, author, senior fellow in *emergent*
(www.emergentvillage.org)

Notes

INTRODUCTION

1. George Barna, "We Have Seen the Future: The Demise of Christianity in Los Angeles County" (Glendale, CA: Barna Research Group, 1990).

ONE
Who Answers God's Mail?

1. Paul Benjamin, *The Equipping Ministry.*
2. John Wimber with Kevin Springer, *Power Evangelism* (San Francisco: Harper & Row, 1986, 2000).

TWO
Unlearning the "E" Word

1. Dudley Lynch and Paul L. Kordis, *Strategy of the Dolphin* (New York: Ballantine, Fawcett Columbine, 1988).
2. Jack Simms, John Wimber, Dave Workman, and Steve Sjogren contributed to these observations.
3. *The Westminster Confession of Faith, An Authentic Modern Version* (Signal Mountain, TN: Summertown, 1979).
4. Rebecca Manley Pippert, *Out of the Saltshaker & Into the World* (Downers Grove, IL: InterVarsity Press, 1979).

THREE
Low Risk, High Grace

1. George Barna, *Ministry Currents,* January-March 1992 (Glendale, CA: Barna Research Group).

FIVE
Five Discoveries That Empower Evangelism

1. St. John of the Cross, *Dark Night of the Soul* (New York: Image, Doubleday, 1959).
2. Gayle D. Erwin, *The Jesus Style* (Waco, TX: Word, 1983), 146.
3. Abridged from T. Trucco, "Serving Mr. Donut and the Community," *The New York Times,* December 26, 1982.
4. C.S. Lewis, *Surprised by Joy* (New York: Inspirational, 1987), 130.

EIGHT
Children Are Naturals

1. Faith Popcorn, *The Popcorn Report* (New York: Doubleday Currency, 1991), 27.

TEN
Displaying the Pearl

1. Laverne Tengborn, "An Historical, Cultural, Geographical, Exegetical Study of Revelation 2 and 3," Doctoral Dissertation for Lutheran Bible Institute, Los Angeles, CA, 1977.